Mind Gardening

A Mental and Physical Health Journal

By Jennifer Groft
Ginkfarfel Press

If found please return to:

_____

_____

Mind Gardening: A Mental and Physical Health Journal

Copyright © 2022 Jennifer Groft

All rights reserved. No portion of this book may be reproduced in any form without permission from the publisher, except as permitted by U.S. copyright law. For permissions contact the author at JenniferGroft.com

Disclaimer: I am not a medical professional, all information and guidance in this book are from journaling strategies I have found helpful in my own path toward better physical and mental health. Part of the purpose of this book is to that you can communicate your symptoms, state of mind, concerns, and progress to the medical professionals taking care of you.

Find me online:
JenniferGroft.com
instagram @JenGroft
Facebook @JenniferGroftWriter
Twitter @GroftJenni
Etsy.com/shop/ginksplace

About this journal:

I designed Mind Gardening: A Mental and Physical Health Journal as a comprehensive, but not time consuming, way of tracking your mental and physical health symptoms. It assists in seeing patterns of behavior and identifying which ones are helpful and which are not. This journal is not meant to replace medical or psychological care, but to aid in communicating with those you might turn to for help. This journal will cover three months if used every day.

Included are:
4 monthly calendars with pre- and post month check ins (4 pages each)
14 weekly planning and check in pages (2 pages each)
98 daily page sets (2 pages each)
Monthly Summaries (right before gratitude prompts)
Gratitude prompts (Last page)

www.ingramcontent.com/pod-product-compliance
Lightning Source LLC
LaVergne TN
LVHW011949060526
838201LV00061B/4262

Types of Pages

Worksheets for discerning Goals and Areas: Goals are things you want to achieve that have specific measurements, starting and stopping points. Areas are those parts of our life that are ongoing but in which we hope to progress. These pages will assist in figuring out how to measure progress and anticipate challenges.

Monthly Page Spread: The Monthly Focus is about identifying ONE THING that will increase your long term health and happiness. You can have other things you are working on, this just sets a top priority. The stars on the days can be used as you choose, to rate your mood, energy, how you did. Or you can just ignore them.

Weekly pages: These are for those wanting a more frequent summary than just monthly. They can also be used as a very basic planner.

Daily Start and Daily End: A series of simple questions for quick journaling and keeping track of mental and physical health, energy levels, and behavior and thought patterns..

Monthly Wrap Up and Weekly Check In: These are the real power of this journal. Take the time to go back over your daily answers and find the patterns in thoughts and behavior. Use this information to adjust expectations, goals, and areas.

Question Examples

Daily, Weekly, and Monthly questions can have answers as short as you want them to be. For example:

What am I interested in or excited about? Starting the new book I just bought
What did I get stuck on yesterday? Watching TV for too long
What progress am I proud of right now? Going for a walk yesterday
Is anything blocking my progress? What is it? Yes, I stayed up too late last night and now I'm overtired.

Primary Goals
Projects with a start and an end

Goal 1:

Why do I want this?

What stands in the way of achieving this goal?

Can I work with these roadblocks or overcome them? How?

Habits or routines that move me toward this goal:

What will it feel like when I achieve this goal?

Goal 2:

Why do I want this?

What stands in the way of achieving this goal?

Can I work with these roadblocks or overcome them? How?

Habits or routines that move me toward this goal:

What will it feel like when I achieve this goal?

Primary Goals
Projects with a start and an end

Goal 3:
  Why do I want this?

  What stands in the way of achieving this goal?

  Can I work with these roadblocks or overcome them? How?

  Habits or routines that move me toward this goal:

  What will it feel like when I achieve this goal?

Areas:
Life elements requiring ongoing maintenance

Area 1:
  How do I want to improve?

  Who will benefit from my efforts in this area? How?

  How will I measure my improvement?

Area 2:
  How do I want to improve?

  Who will benefit from my efforts in this area? How?

  How will I measure my improvement?

Monthly Warm Up

Month:
How am I right now?
  Mental:

  Emotional:

  Physical:

  Spiritual:

Recent Positives:

Recent Negatives:

Current Stresses or Energy Drains:

In the coming month...
  I want to do less:

  I want to do more:

  I want to feel:

  To feel this way I will:

  If I get stuck I will remember:

Month:

Focus:

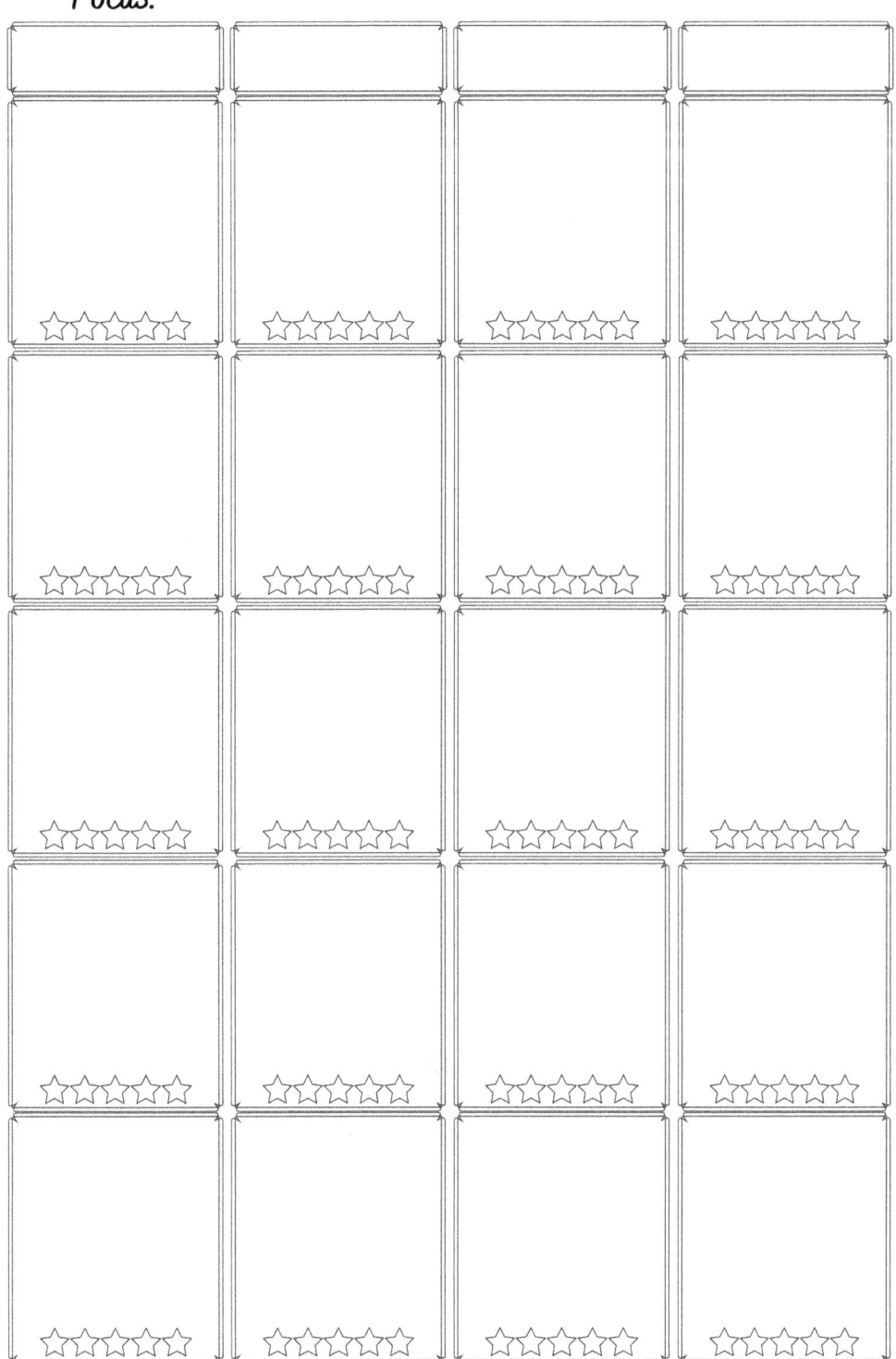

Monthly Wrap Up

Month:
What worked well?

What needed improvement?

Progress on Goals:
1.
2.
3.

Progress on Areas:
1.

2.

Patterns:
Top 3 things I was interested in or excited about:
1.
2.
3.

Top 3 things I got stuck on or that blocked my progress:
1.
2.
3.

What do these patterns tell me?

Other Notes:

Monthly Warm Up

Month:
How am I right now?
  Mental:

  Emotional:

  Physical:

  Spiritual:

Recent Positives:

Recent Negatives:

Current Stresses or Energy Drains:

In the coming month...
  I want to do less:

  I want to do more:

  I want to feel:

  To feel this way I will:

  If I get stuck I will remember:

Month:

Focus:

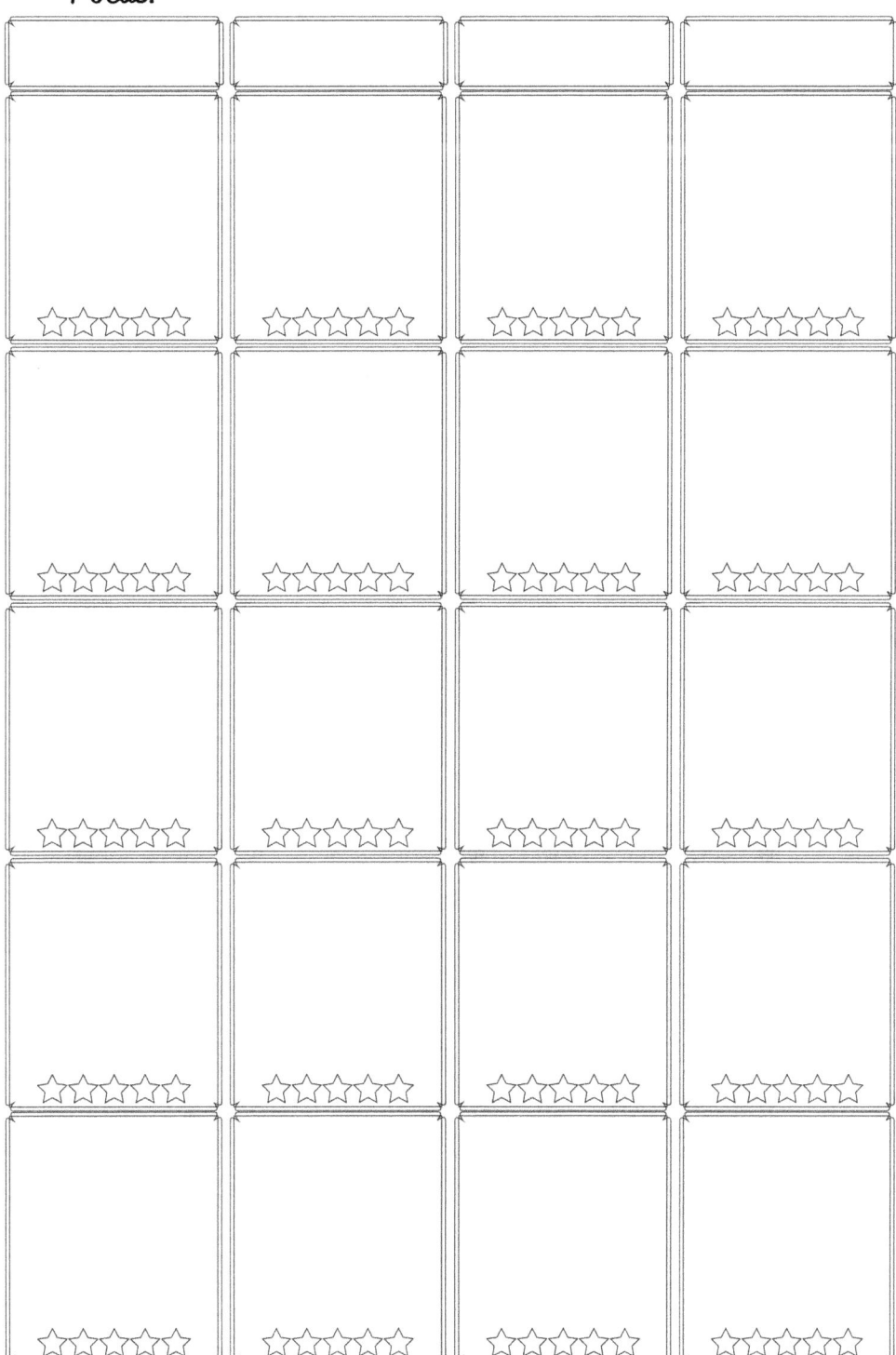

Monthly Wrap Up

Month:

What worked well?

What needed improvement?

Progress on Goals:
1.
2.
3.

Progress on Areas:
1.

2.

Patterns:
Top 3 things I was interested in or excited about:
1.
2.
3.

Top 3 things I got stuck on or that blocked my progress:
1.
2.
3.

What do these patterns tell me?

Other Notes:

Monthly Warm Up

Month:
How am I right now?
  Mental:

  Emotional:

  Physical:

  Spiritual:

Recent Positives:

Recent Negatives:

Current Stresses or Energy Drains:

In the coming month...
  I want to do less:

  I want to do more:

  I want to feel:

  To feel this way I will:

  If I get stuck I will remember:

Month:

Focus:

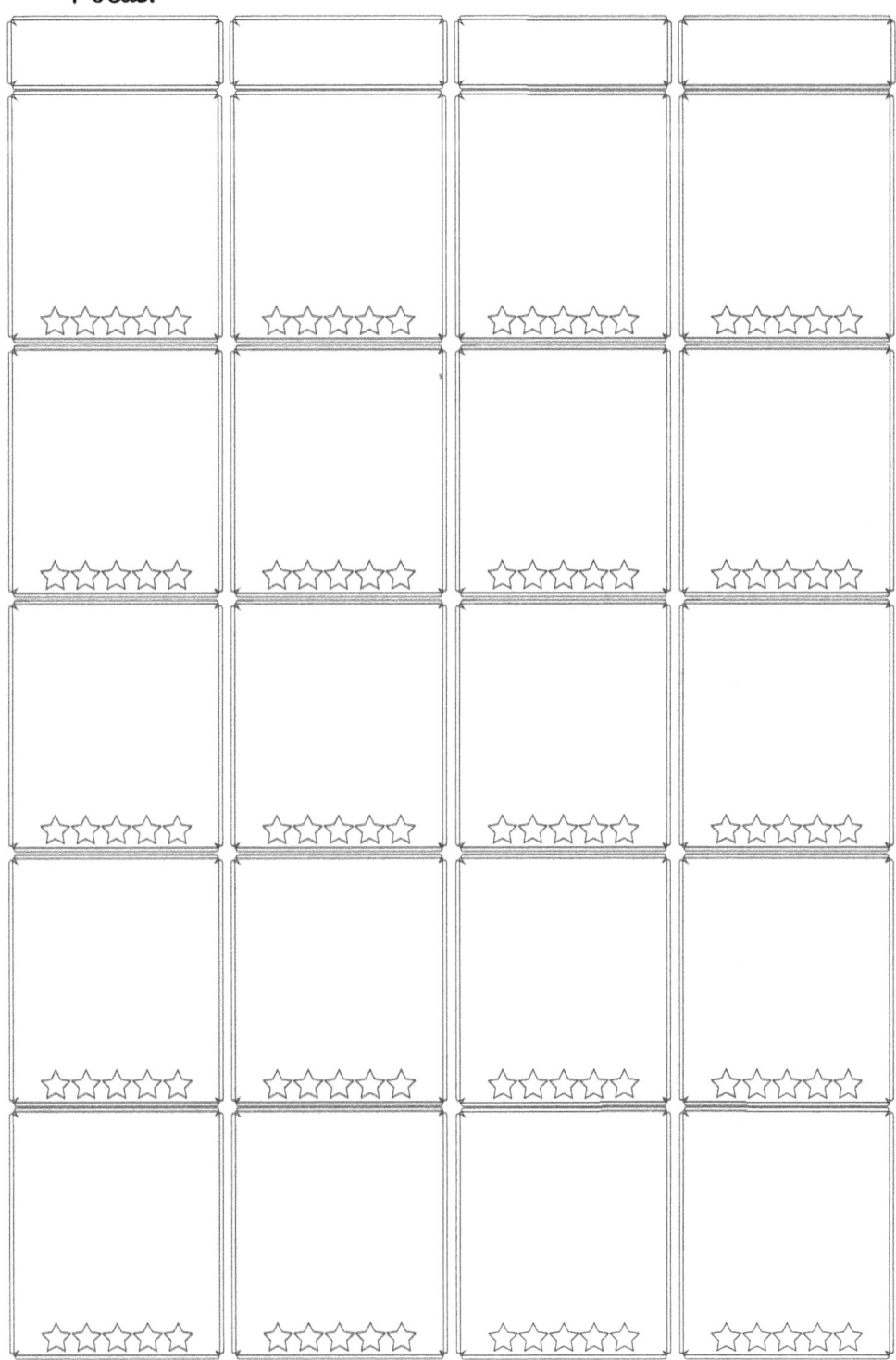

Monthly Wrap Up

Month:

What worked well?

What needed improvement?

Progress on Goals:
1.
2.
3.

Progress on Areas:
1.

2.

Patterns:
Top 3 things I was interested in or excited about:
1.
2.
3.

Top 3 things I got stuck on or that blocked my progress:
1.
2.
3.

What do these patterns tell me?

Other Notes:

Monthly Warm Up

Month:
How am I right now?
  Mental:

  Emotional:

  Physical:

  Spiritual:

Recent Positives:

Recent Negatives:

Current Stresses or Energy Drains:

In the coming month...
  I want to do less:

  I want to do more:

  I want to feel:

  To feel this way I will:

  If I get stuck I will remember:

Month:

Focus:

Monthly Wrap Up

Month:

What worked well?

What needed improvement?

Progress on Goals:
1.
2.
3.

Progress on Areas:
1.

2.

Patterns:
Top 3 things I was interested in or excited about:
1.
2.
3.

Top 3 things I got stuck on or that blocked my progress:
1.
2.
3.

What do these patterns tell me?

Other Notes:

This Week

Top goals this week
-
-
-
-
-

How can I make this week great?

For mental and emotional health I will:

For physical health I will:

For spiritual health I will:

For intellectual health I will:

Weekly Check In

Dates:

What worked well?

What needed improvement?

Progress on Goals:
1.
2.
3.

Progress on Areas:
1.

2.

Patterns:
Top 3 things I was interested in or excited about:
1.
2.
3.

Top 3 things I got stuck on or that blocked my progress:
1.
2.
3.

What do these patterns tell me?

Other Notes:

This Week

Top goals this week
-
-
-
-
-

How can I make this week great?

For mental and emotional health I will:

For physical health I will:

For spiritual health I will:

For intellectual health I will:

Weekly Check In

Dates:
What worked well?

What needed improvement?

Progress on Goals:
1.
2.
3.

Progress on Areas:
1.

2.

Patterns:
Top 3 things I was interested in or excited about:
1.
2.
3.

Top 3 things I got stuck on or that blocked my progress:
1.
2.
3.

What do these patterns tell me?

Other Notes:

This Week

Top goals this week
-
-
-
-
-

How can I make this week great?

For mental and emotional health I will:

For physical health I will:

For spiritual health I will:

For intellectual health I will:

Weekly Check In

Dates:

What worked well?

What needed improvement?

Progress on Goals:
1.
2.
3.

Progress on Areas:
1.

2.

Patterns:
Top 3 things I was interested in or excited about:
1.
2.
3.

Top 3 things I got stuck on or that blocked my progress:
1.
2.
3.

What do these patterns tell me?

Other Notes:

This Week

Top goals this week
-
-
-
-
-

How can I make this week great?

For mental and emotional health I will:

For physical health I will:

For spiritual health I will:

For intellectual health I will:

Weekly Check In

Dates:

What worked well?

What needed improvement?

Progress on Goals:
1.
2.
3.

Progress on Areas:
1.

2.

Patterns:
Top 3 things I was interested in or excited about:
1.
2.
3.

Top 3 things I got stuck on or that blocked my progress:
1.
2.
3.

What do these patterns tell me?

Other Notes:

This Week

Top goals this week
-
-
-
-
-

How can I make this week great?
....
....
....
....

For mental and emotional health I will:
....

For physical health I will:
....

For spiritual health I will:
....

For intellectual health I will:
....

Weekly Check In

Dates:
What worked well?

What needed improvement?

Progress on Goals:
1.
2.
3.

Progress on Areas:
1.

2.

Patterns:
Top 3 things I was interested in or excited about:
1.
2.
3.

Top 3 things I got stuck on or that blocked my progress:
1.
2.
3.

What do these patterns tell me?

Other Notes:

This Week

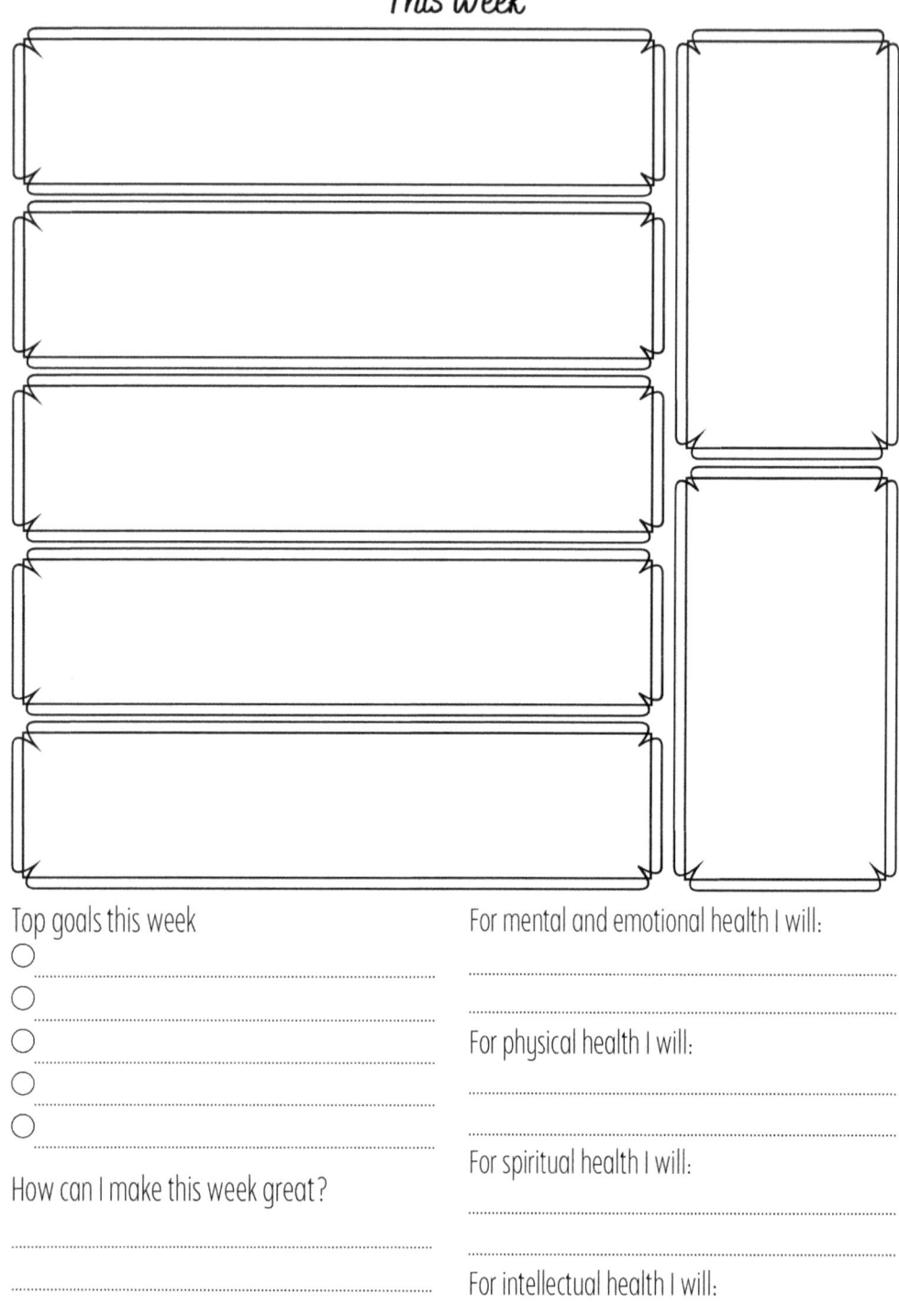

Top goals this week
-
-
-
-
-

How can I make this week great?
....
....
....

For mental and emotional health I will:
....

For physical health I will:
....

For spiritual health I will:
....

For intellectual health I will:
....

Weekly Check In

Dates:

What worked well?

What needed improvement?

Progress on Goals:
1.
2.
3.

Progress on Areas:
1.

2.

Patterns:
Top 3 things I was interested in or excited about:
1.
2.
3.

Top 3 things I got stuck on or that blocked my progress:
1.
2.
3.

What do these patterns tell me?

Other Notes:

This Week

Top goals this week
- ○
- ○
- ○
- ○
- ○

How can I make this week great?

For mental and emotional health I will:

For physical health I will:

For spiritual health I will:

For intellectual health I will:

Weekly Check In

Dates:

What worked well?

What needed improvement?

Progress on Goals:
1.
2.
3.

Progress on Areas:
1.

2.

Patterns:
Top 3 things I was interested in or excited about:
1.
2.
3.

Top 3 things I got stuck on or that blocked my progress:
1.
2.
3.

What do these patterns tell me?

Other Notes:

This Week

Top goals this week
-
-
-
-
-

How can I make this week great?

For mental and emotional health I will:

For physical health I will:

For spiritual health I will:

For intellectual health I will:

Weekly Check In

Dates:

What worked well?

What needed improvement?

Progress on Goals:
1.
2.
3.

Progress on Areas:
1.

2.

Patterns:
Top 3 things I was interested in or excited about:
1.
2.
3.

Top 3 things I got stuck on or that blocked my progress:
1.
2.
3.

What do these patterns tell me?

Other Notes:

This Week

Top goals this week
-
-
-
-
-

How can I make this week great?

For mental and emotional health I will:

For physical health I will:

For spiritual health I will:

For intellectual health I will:

Weekly Check In

Dates:

What worked well?

What needed improvement?

Progress on Goals:
1.
2.
3.

Progress on Areas:
1.

2.

Patterns:
Top 3 things I was interested in or excited about:
1.
2.
3.

Top 3 things I got stuck on or that blocked my progress:
1.
2.
3.

What do these patterns tell me?

Other Notes:

This Week

Top goals this week
-
-
-
-
-

How can I make this week great?
....
....
....
....

For mental and emotional health I will:
....
....

For physical health I will:
....
....

For spiritual health I will:
....
....

For intellectual health I will:
....
....

Weekly Check In

Dates:

What worked well?

What needed improvement?

Progress on Goals:
1.
2.
3.

Progress on Areas:
1.

2.

Patterns:
Top 3 things I was interested in or excited about:
1.
2.
3.

Top 3 things I got stuck on or that blocked my progress:
1.
2.
3.

What do these patterns tell me?

Other Notes:

This Week

Top goals this week
- ....
- ....
- ....
- ....
- ....

How can I make this week great?
....
....
....
....

For mental and emotional health I will:
....
....

For physical health I will:
....
....

For spiritual health I will:
....
....

For intellectual health I will:
....
....

Weekly Check In

Dates:

What worked well?

What needed improvement?

Progress on Goals:
1.
2.
3.

Progress on Areas:
1.

2.

Patterns:
Top 3 things I was interested in or excited about:
1.
2.
3.

Top 3 things I got stuck on or that blocked my progress:
1.
2.
3.

What do these patterns tell me?

Other Notes:

This Week

Top goals this week
-
-
-
-
-

How can I make this week great?
....
....
....
....

For mental and emotional health I will:
....
....

For physical health I will:
....
....

For spiritual health I will:
....
....

For intellectual health I will:
....
....

Weekly Check In

Dates:

What worked well?

What needed improvement?

Progress on Goals:
1.
2.
3.

Progress on Areas:
1.

2.

Patterns:
Top 3 things I was interested in or excited about:
1.
2.
3.

Top 3 things I got stuck on or that blocked my progress:
1.
2.
3.

What do these patterns tell me?

Other Notes:

This Week

Top goals this week
-
-
-
-
-

How can I make this week great?

For mental and emotional health I will:

For physical health I will:

For spiritual health I will:

For intellectual health I will:

Weekly Check In

Dates:

What worked well?

What needed improvement?

Progress on Goals:
1.
2.
3.

Progress on Areas:
1.

2.

Patterns:
Top 3 things I was interested in or excited about:
1.
2.
3.

Top 3 things I got stuck on or that blocked my progress:
1.
2.
3.

What do these patterns tell me?

Other Notes:

This Week

Top goals this week
-
-
-
-
-

How can I make this week great?

For mental and emotional health I will:

For physical health I will:

For spiritual health I will:

For intellectual health I will:

Weekly Check In

Dates:

What worked well?

What needed improvement?

Progress on Goals:
1.
2.
3.

Progress on Areas:
1.

2.

Patterns:
Top 3 things I was interested in or excited about:
1.
2.
3.

Top 3 things I got stuck on or that blocked my progress:
1.
2.
3.

What do these patterns tell me?

Other Notes:

Daily Start

Date: Current time:

How did I sleep?

What did I think or feel when I woke up?

Energy Level: 1 - 2 - 3 - 4 - 5 - 6 - 7 - 8 - 9 - 10

What am I interested in or excited about?

What did I get stuck on yesterday?

What progress am I proud of right now?

Is anything blocking my progress? What is it?

Things to do brain dump:

What is one thing I will definitely achieve today?

What is one thing I would love to do today?

Gratitude:
1.
2.
3.

Notes and Plans:

Daily End

Date: Current time:

What went well today?

What needs improvement?

Something I learned today:

What did I read, watch, or listen to?

Daily Summary Cues

Where did I go?

Who did I interact with?

How did people, my location, or the weather impact me?

Something that made me happy:

Any changes brewing?

Daily Summary: (free write)

Health Notes:
Physical Symptoms:

Breakfast:

Lunch:

Dinner:

Exercise:

Snacks:

Water:
Weight:

Daily Start

Date: Current time:

How did I sleep?

What did I think or feel when I woke up?

Energy Level: 1 - 2 - 3 - 4 - 5 - 6 - 7 - 8 - 9 - 10

What am I interested in or excited about?

What did I get stuck on yesterday?

What progress am I proud of right now?

Is anything blocking my progress? What is it?

Things to do brain dump:

What is one thing I will definitely achieve today?

What is one thing I would love to do today?

Gratitude:
1.
2.
3.

Notes and Plans:

Daily End

Date: Current time:

What went well today?

What needs improvement?

Something I learned today:

What did I read, watch, or listen to?

Daily Summary Cues

Where did I go?

Who did I interact with?

How did people, my location, or the weather impact me?

Something that made me happy:

Any changes brewing?

Daily Summary: (free write)

Health Notes:
Physical Symptoms: Breakfast:

                                       Lunch:

                                       Dinner:

Exercise:
                                       Snacks:

Water:
Weight:

Daily Start

Date: Current time:

How did I sleep?

What did I think or feel when I woke up?

Energy Level: 1 - 2 - 3 - 4 - 5 - 6 - 7 - 8 - 9 - 10

What am I interested in or excited about?

What did I get stuck on yesterday?

What progress am I proud of right now?

Is anything blocking my progress? What is it?

Things to do brain dump:

What is one thing I will definitely achieve today?

What is one thing I would love to do today?

Gratitude:
1.
2.
3.

Notes and Plans:

Daily End

Date: Current time:

What went well today?

What needs improvement?

Something I learned today:

What did I read, watch, or listen to?

Daily Summary Cues
- Where did I go?
- Who did I interact with?
- How did people, my location, or the weather impact me?
- Something that made me happy:
- Any changes brewing?

Daily Summary: (free write)

Health Notes:
Physical Symptoms: Breakfast:

                                       Lunch:

                                       Dinner:

Exercise: Snacks:

Water:
Weight:

Daily Start

Date: Current time:

How did I sleep?

What did I think or feel when I woke up?

Energy Level: 1 - 2 - 3 - 4 - 5 - 6 - 7 - 8 - 9 - 10

What am I interested in or excited about?

What did I get stuck on yesterday?

What progress am I proud of right now?

Is anything blocking my progress? What is it?

Things to do brain dump:

What is one thing I will definitely achieve today?

What is one thing I would love to do today?

Gratitude:
1.
2.
3.

Notes and Plans:

Daily End

Date: Current time:

What went well today?

What needs improvement?

Something I learned today:

What did I read, watch, or listen to?

Daily Summary Cues

Where did I go?

Who did I interact with?

How did people, my location, or the weather impact me?

Something that made me happy:

Any changes brewing?

Daily Summary: (free write)

Health Notes:
Physical Symptoms: Breakfast:

                                     Lunch:

                                     Dinner:
Exercise:
                                     Snacks:

Water:
Weight:

Daily Start

Date: Current time:

How did I sleep?

What did I think or feel when I woke up?

Energy Level: 1 - 2 - 3 - 4 - 5 - 6 - 7 - 8 - 9 - 10

What am I interested in or excited about?

What did I get stuck on yesterday?

What progress am I proud of right now?

Is anything blocking my progress? What is it?

Things to do brain dump:

What is one thing I will definitely achieve today?

What is one thing I would love to do today?

Gratitude:
1.
2.
3.

Notes and Plans:

Daily End

Date: Current time:

What went well today?

What needs improvement?

Something I learned today:

What did I read, watch, or listen to?

Daily Summary Cues

Where did I go?

Who did I interact with?

How did people, my location, or the weather impact me?

Something that made me happy:

Any changes brewing?

Daily Summary: (free write)

Health Notes:
Physical Symptoms: Breakfast:

                                      Lunch:

                                      Dinner:

Exercise: Snacks:

Water:
Weight:

Daily Start

Date: Current time:

How did I sleep?

What did I think or feel when I woke up?

Energy Level: 1 - 2 - 3 - 4 - 5 - 6 - 7 - 8 - 9 - 10

What am I interested in or excited about?

What did I get stuck on yesterday?

What progress am I proud of right now?

Is anything blocking my progress? What is it?

Things to do brain dump:

What is one thing I will definitely achieve today?

What is one thing I would love to do today?

Gratitude:
1.
2.
3.

Notes and Plans:

Daily End

Date: Current time:

What went well today?

What needs improvement?

Something I learned today:

What did I read, watch, or listen to?

Daily Summary Cues

Where did I go?

Who did I interact with?

How did people, my location, or the weather impact me?

Something that made me happy:

Any changes brewing?

Daily Summary: (free write)

Health Notes:
Physical Symptoms: Breakfast:

                                         Lunch:

                                         Dinner:
Exercise:
                                         Snacks:

Water:
Weight:

Daily Start

Date: Current time:

How did I sleep?

What did I think or feel when I woke up?

Energy Level: 1 - 2 - 3 - 4 - 5 - 6 - 7 - 8 - 9 - 10

What am I interested in or excited about?

What did I get stuck on yesterday?

What progress am I proud of right now?

Is anything blocking my progress? What is it?

Things to do brain dump:

What is one thing I will definitely achieve today?

What is one thing I would love to do today?

Gratitude:
1.
2.
3.

Notes and Plans:

Daily End

Date: Current time:

What went well today?

What needs improvement?

Something I learned today:

What did I read, watch, or listen to?

Daily Summary Cues

Where did I go?

Who did I interact with?

How did people, my location, or the weather impact me?

Something that made me happy:

Any changes brewing?

Daily Summary: (free write)

Health Notes:
Physical Symptoms:

Exercise:

Water:
Weight:

Breakfast:

Lunch:

Dinner:

Snacks:

Daily Start

Date: Current time:

How did I sleep?

What did I think or feel when I woke up?

Energy Level: 1 - 2 - 3 - 4 - 5 - 6 - 7 - 8 - 9 - 10

What am I interested in or excited about?

What did I get stuck on yesterday?

What progress am I proud of right now?

Is anything blocking my progress? What is it?

Things to do brain dump:

What is one thing I will definitely achieve today?

What is one thing I would love to do today?

Gratitude:
1.
2.
3.

Notes and Plans:

Daily End

Date: Current time:

What went well today?

What needs improvement?

Something I learned today:

What did I read, watch, or listen to?

Daily Summary Cues

- Where did I go?
- Who did I interact with?
- How did people, my location, or the weather impact me?
- Something that made me happy:
- Any changes brewing?

Daily Summary: (free write)

Health Notes:
Physical Symptoms: Breakfast:

                                        Lunch:

                                        Dinner:

Exercise:
                                        Snacks:

Water:
Weight:

Daily Start

Date: Current time:

How did I sleep?

What did I think or feel when I woke up?

Energy Level: 1 - 2 - 3 - 4 - 5 - 6 - 7 - 8 - 9 - 10

What am I interested in or excited about?

What did I get stuck on yesterday?

What progress am I proud of right now?

Is anything blocking my progress? What is it?

Things to do brain dump:

What is one thing I will definitely achieve today?

What is one thing I would love to do today?

Gratitude:
1.
2.
3.

Notes and Plans:

Daily End

Date: Current time:

What went well today?

What needs improvement?

Something I learned today:

What did I read, watch, or listen to?

Daily Summary Cues

- Where did I go?
- Who did I interact with?
- How did people, my location, or the weather impact me?
- Something that made me happy:
- Any changes brewing?

Daily Summary: (free write)

Health Notes:
Physical Symptoms: Breakfast:

                                   Lunch:

                                   Dinner:

Exercise: Snacks:

Water:
Weight:

Daily Start

Date: Current time:

How did I sleep?

What did I think or feel when I woke up?

Energy Level: 1 - 2 - 3 - 4 - 5 - 6 - 7 - 8 - 9 - 10

What am I interested in or excited about?

What did I get stuck on yesterday?

What progress am I proud of right now?

Is anything blocking my progress? What is it?

Things to do brain dump:

What is one thing I will definitely achieve today?

What is one thing I would love to do today?

Gratitude:
1.
2.
3.

Notes and Plans:

Daily End

Date: Current time:

What went well today?

What needs improvement?

Something I learned today:

What did I read, watch, or listen to?

Daily Summary Cues

Where did I go?

Who did I interact with?

How did people, my location, or the weather impact me?

Something that made me happy:

Any changes brewing?

Daily Summary: (free write)

Health Notes:
Physical Symptoms:

Breakfast:

Lunch:

Dinner:

Exercise:

Snacks:

Water:
Weight:

Daily Start

Date: Current time:

How did I sleep?

What did I think or feel when I woke up?

Energy Level: 1 - 2 - 3 - 4 - 5 - 6 - 7 - 8 - 9 - 10

What am I interested in or excited about?

What did I get stuck on yesterday?

What progress am I proud of right now?

Is anything blocking my progress? What is it?

Things to do brain dump:

What is one thing I will definitely achieve today?

What is one thing I would love to do today?

Gratitude:
1.
2.
3.

Notes and Plans:

Daily End

Date: Current time:

What went well today?

What needs improvement?

Something I learned today:

What did I read, watch, or listen to?

Daily Summary Cues

Where did I go?

Who did I interact with?

How did people, my location, or the weather impact me?

Something that made me happy:

Any changes brewing?

Daily Summary: (free write)

Health Notes:
Physical Symptoms:

Breakfast:

Lunch:

Dinner:

Exercise:

Snacks:

Water:
Weight:

Daily Start

Date: Current time:

How did I sleep?

What did I think or feel when I woke up?

Energy Level: 1 - 2 - 3 - 4 - 5 - 6 - 7 - 8 - 9 - 10

What am I interested in or excited about?

What did I get stuck on yesterday?

What progress am I proud of right now?

Is anything blocking my progress? What is it?

Things to do brain dump:

What is one thing I will definitely achieve today?

What is one thing I would love to do today?

Gratitude:
1.
2.
3.

Notes and Plans:

Daily End

Date: Current time:

What went well today?

What needs improvement?

Something I learned today:

What did I read, watch, or listen to?

Daily Summary Cues

Where did I go?

Who did I interact with?

How did people, my location, or the weather impact me?

Something that made me happy:

Any changes brewing?

Daily Summary: (free write)

Health Notes:
Physical Symptoms: Breakfast:

                                       Lunch:

                                       Dinner:

Exercise:
                                       Snacks:

Water:
Weight:

Daily Start

Date: Current time:

How did I sleep?

What did I think or feel when I woke up?

Energy Level: 1 - 2 - 3 - 4 - 5 - 6 - 7 - 8 - 9 - 10

What am I interested in or excited about?

What did I get stuck on yesterday?

What progress am I proud of right now?

Is anything blocking my progress? What is it?

Things to do brain dump:

What is one thing I will definitely achieve today?

What is one thing I would love to do today?

Gratitude:
1.
2.
3.

Notes and Plans:

Daily End

Date: Current time:

What went well today?

What needs improvement?

Something I learned today:

What did I read, watch, or listen to?

Daily Summary Cues

Where did I go?

Who did I interact with?

How did people, my location, or the weather impact me?

Something that made me happy:

Any changes brewing?

Daily Summary: (free write)

Health Notes:
Physical Symptoms: Breakfast:

                                     Lunch:

                                     Dinner:

Exercise:
                                     Snacks:

Water:
Weight:

Daily Start

Date: Current time:

How did I sleep?

What did I think or feel when I woke up?

Energy Level: 1 - 2 - 3 - 4 - 5 - 6 - 7 - 8 - 9 - 10

What am I interested in or excited about?

What did I get stuck on yesterday?

What progress am I proud of right now?

Is anything blocking my progress? What is it?

Things to do brain dump:

What is one thing I will definitely achieve today?

What is one thing I would love to do today?

Gratitude:
1.
2.
3.

Notes and Plans:

Daily End

Date: Current time:

What went well today?

What needs improvement?

Something I learned today:

What did I read, watch, or listen to?

Daily Summary Cues

Where did I go?

Who did I interact with?

How did people, my location, or the weather impact me?

Something that made me happy:

Any changes brewing?

Daily Summary: (free write)

Health Notes:
Physical Symptoms:

Breakfast:

Lunch:

Dinner:

Exercise:

Snacks:

Water:
Weight:

Daily Start

Date: Current time:

How did I sleep?

What did I think or feel when I woke up?

Energy Level: 1 - 2 - 3 - 4 - 5 - 6 - 7 - 8 - 9 - 10

What am I interested in or excited about?

What did I get stuck on yesterday?

What progress am I proud of right now?

Is anything blocking my progress? What is it?

Things to do brain dump:

What is one thing I will definitely achieve today?

What is one thing I would love to do today?

Gratitude:
1.
2.
3.

Notes and Plans:

Daily End

Date: Current time:

What went well today?

What needs improvement?

Something I learned today:

What did I read, watch, or listen to?

Daily Summary Cues

Where did I go?

Who did I interact with?

How did people, my location, or the weather impact me?

Something that made me happy:

Any changes brewing?

Daily Summary: (free write)

Health Notes:
Physical Symptoms:

Exercise:

Water:
Weight:

Breakfast:

Lunch:

Dinner:

Snacks:

Daily Start

Date: Current time:

How did I sleep?

What did I think or feel when I woke up?

Energy Level: 1 - 2 - 3 - 4 - 5 - 6 - 7 - 8 - 9 - 10

What am I interested in or excited about?

What did I get stuck on yesterday?

What progress am I proud of right now?

Is anything blocking my progress? What is it?

Things to do brain dump:

What is one thing I will definitely achieve today?

What is one thing I would love to do today?

Gratitude:
1.
2.
3.

Notes and Plans:

Daily End

Date: Current time:

What went well today?

What needs improvement?

Something I learned today:

What did I read, watch, or listen to?

Daily Summary Cues

Where did I go?

Who did I interact with?

How did people, my location, or the weather impact me?

Something that made me happy:

Any changes brewing?

Daily Summary: (free write)

Health Notes:
Physical Symptoms: Breakfast:

Lunch:

Dinner:

Exercise: Snacks:

Water:
Weight:

Daily Start

Date: Current time:

How did I sleep?

What did I think or feel when I woke up?

Energy Level: 1 - 2 - 3 - 4 - 5 - 6 - 7 - 8 - 9 - 10

What am I interested in or excited about?

What did I get stuck on yesterday?

What progress am I proud of right now?

Is anything blocking my progress? What is it?

Things to do brain dump:

What is one thing I will definitely achieve today?

What is one thing I would love to do today?

Gratitude:
1.
2.
3.

Notes and Plans:

Daily End

Date: Current time:

What went well today?

What needs improvement?

Something I learned today:

What did I read, watch, or listen to?

Daily Summary Cues

Where did I go?

Who did I interact with?

How did people, my location, or the weather impact me?

Something that made me happy:

Any changes brewing?

Daily Summary: (free write)

Health Notes:
Physical Symptoms: Breakfast:

                                         Lunch:

                                         Dinner:
Exercise:
                                         Snacks:

Water:
Weight:

Daily Start

Date: Current time:

How did I sleep?

What did I think or feel when I woke up?

Energy Level: 1 - 2 - 3 - 4 - 5 - 6 - 7 - 8 - 9 - 10

What am I interested in or excited about?

What did I get stuck on yesterday?

What progress am I proud of right now?

Is anything blocking my progress? What is it?

Things to do brain dump:

What is one thing I will definitely achieve today?

What is one thing I would love to do today?

Gratitude:
1.
2.
3.

Notes and Plans:

Daily End

Date: Current time:

What went well today?

What needs improvement?

Something I learned today:

What did I read, watch, or listen to?

Daily Summary Cues

- Where did I go?
- Who did I interact with?
- How did people, my location, or the weather impact me?
- Something that made me happy:
- Any changes brewing?

Daily Summary: (free write)

Health Notes:
Physical Symptoms: Breakfast:

                                         Lunch:

                                         Dinner:

Exercise: Snacks:

Water:
Weight:

Daily Start

Date: Current time:

How did I sleep?

What did I think or feel when I woke up?

Energy Level: 1 - 2 - 3 - 4 - 5 - 6 - 7 - 8 - 9 - 10

What am I interested in or excited about?

What did I get stuck on yesterday?

What progress am I proud of right now?

Is anything blocking my progress? What is it?

Things to do brain dump:

What is one thing I will definitely achieve today?

What is one thing I would love to do today?

Gratitude:
1.
2.
3.

Notes and Plans:

Daily End

Date: Current time:

What went well today?

What needs improvement?

Something I learned today:

What did I read, watch, or listen to?

Daily Summary Cues

Where did I go?

Who did I interact with?

How did people, my location, or the weather impact me?

Something that made me happy:

Any changes brewing?

Daily Summary: (free write)

Health Notes:
Physical Symptoms: Breakfast:

                                    Lunch:

                                    Dinner:
Exercise:
                                    Snacks:

Water:
Weight:

Daily Start

Date: Current time:

How did I sleep?

What did I think or feel when I woke up?

Energy Level: 1 - 2 - 3 - 4 - 5 - 6 - 7 - 8 - 9 - 10

What am I interested in, or excited about?

What did I get stuck on yesterday?

What progress am I proud of right now?

Is anything blocking my progress? What is it?

Things to do brain dump:

What is one thing I will definitely achieve today?

What is one thing I would love to do today?

Gratitude:
1.
2.
3.

Notes and Plans:

Daily End

Date: Current time:

What went well today?

What needs improvement?

Something I learned today:

What did I read, watch, or listen to?

Daily Summary Cues

Where did I go?

Who did I interact with?

How did people, my location, or the weather impact me?

Something that made me happy:

Any changes brewing?

Daily Summary: (free write)

Health Notes:
Physical Symptoms:

Breakfast:

Lunch:

Dinner:

Exercise:

Snacks:

Water:
Weight:

Daily Start

Date: Current time:

How did I sleep?

What did I think or feel when I woke up?

Energy Level: 1 - 2 - 3 - 4 - 5 - 6 - 7 - 8 - 9 - 10

What am I interested in or excited about?

What did I get stuck on yesterday?

What progress am I proud of right now?

Is anything blocking my progress? What is it?

Things to do brain dump:

What is one thing I will definitely achieve today?

What is one thing I would love to do today?

Gratitude:
1.
2.
3.

Notes and Plans:

Daily End

Date: Current time:

What went well today?

What needs improvement?

Something I learned today:

What did I read, watch, or listen to?

Daily Summary Cues
- Where did I go?
- Who did I interact with?
- How did people, my location, or the weather impact me?
- Something that made me happy:
- Any changes brewing?

Daily Summary: (free write)

Health Notes:
Physical Symptoms: Breakfast:

                                         Lunch:

                                         Dinner:
Exercise:
                                         Snacks:

Water:
Weight:

Daily Start

Date: Current time:

How did I sleep?

What did I think or feel when I woke up?

Energy Level: 1 - 2 - 3 - 4 - 5 - 6 - 7 - 8 - 9 - 10

What am I interested in or excited about?

What did I get stuck on yesterday?

What progress am I proud of right now?

Is anything blocking my progress? What is it?

Things to do brain dump:

What is one thing I will definitely achieve today?

What is one thing I would love to do today?

Gratitude:
1.
2.
3.

Notes and Plans:

Daily End

Date: Current time:

What went well today?

What needs improvement?

Something I learned today:

What did I read, watch, or listen to?

Daily Summary Cues

Where did I go?

Who did I interact with?

How did people, my location, or the weather impact me?

Something that made me happy:

Any changes brewing?

Daily Summary: (free write)

Health Notes:
Physical Symptoms: Breakfast:

                                       Lunch:

                                       Dinner:
Exercise:
                                       Snacks:

Water:
Weight:

Daily Start

Date: Current time:

How did I sleep?

What did I think or feel when I woke up?

Energy Level: 1 - 2 - 3 - 4 - 5 - 6 - 7 - 8 - 9 - 10

What am I interested in, or excited about?

What did I get stuck on yesterday?

What progress am I proud of right now?

Is anything blocking my progress? What is it?

Things to do brain dump:

What is one thing I will definitely achieve today?

What is one thing I would love to do today?

Gratitude:
1.
2.
3.

Notes and Plans:

Daily End

Date: Current time:

What went well today?

What needs improvement?

Something I learned today:

What did I read, watch, or listen to?

Daily Summary Cues

Where did I go?

Who did I interact with?

How did people, my location, or the weather impact me?

Something that made me happy:

Any changes brewing?

Daily Summary: (free write)

Health Notes:
Physical Symptoms: Breakfast:

                                      Lunch:

                                      Dinner:

Exercise:
                                      Snacks:

Water:
Weight:

Daily Start

Date: Current time:

How did I sleep?

What did I think or feel when I woke up?

Energy Level: 1 - 2 - 3 - 4 - 5 - 6 - 7 - 8 - 9 - 10

What am I interested in or excited about?

What did I get stuck on yesterday?

What progress am I proud of right now?

Is anything blocking my progress? What is it?

Things to do brain dump:

What is one thing I will definitely achieve today?

What is one thing I would love to do today?

Gratitude:
1.
2.
3.

Notes and Plans:

Daily End

Date: Current time:

What went well today?

What needs improvement?

Something I learned today:

What did I read, watch, or listen to?

Daily Summary Cues

Where did I go?

Who did I interact with?

How did people, my location, or the weather impact me?

Something that made me happy:

Any changes brewing?

Daily Summary: (free write)

Health Notes:
Physical Symptoms: Breakfast:

                                        Lunch:

                                        Dinner:

Exercise: Snacks:

Water:
Weight:

Daily Start

Date: Current time:

How did I sleep?

What did I think or feel when I woke up?

Energy Level: 1 - 2 - 3 - 4 - 5 - 6 - 7 - 8 - 9 - 10

What am I interested in or excited about?

What did I get stuck on yesterday?

What progress am I proud of right now?

Is anything blocking my progress? What is it?

Things to do brain dump:

What is one thing I will definitely achieve today?

What is one thing I would love to do today?

Gratitude:
1.
2.
3.

Notes and Plans:

Daily End

Date: Current time:

What went well today?

What needs improvement?

Something I learned today:

What did I read, watch, or listen to?

Daily Summary Cues

Where did I go?

Who did I interact with?

How did people, my location, or the weather impact me?

Something that made me happy:

Any changes brewing?

Daily Summary: (free write)

Health Notes:
Physical Symptoms: Breakfast:

                                   Lunch:

                                   Dinner:

Exercise:
                                   Snacks:

Water:
Weight:

Daily Start

Date: Current time:

How did I sleep?

What did I think or feel when I woke up?

Energy Level: 1 - 2 - 3 - 4 - 5 - 6 - 7 - 8 - 9 - 10

What am I interested in or excited about?

What did I get stuck on yesterday?

What progress am I proud of right now?

Is anything blocking my progress? What is it?

Things to do brain dump:

What is one thing I will definitely achieve today?

What is one thing I would love to do today?

Gratitude:
1.
2.
3.

Notes and Plans:

Daily End

Date: Current time:

What went well today?

What needs improvement?

Something I learned today:

What did I read, watch, or listen to?

Daily Summary Cues

Where did I go?

Who did I interact with?

How did people, my location, or the weather impact me?

Something that made me happy:

Any changes brewing?

Daily Summary: (free write)

Health Notes:
Physical Symptoms:

Breakfast:

Lunch:

Dinner:

Exercise:

Snacks:

Water:
Weight:

Daily Start

Date: Current time:

How did I sleep?

What did I think or feel when I woke up?

Energy Level: 1 - 2 - 3 - 4 - 5 - 6 - 7 - 8 - 9 - 10

What am I interested in or excited about?

What did I get stuck on yesterday?

What progress am I proud of right now?

Is anything blocking my progress? What is it?

Things to do brain dump:

What is one thing I will definitely achieve today?

What is one thing I would love to do today?

Gratitude:
1.
2.
3.

Notes and Plans:

Daily End

Date: Current time:

What went well today?

What needs improvement?

Something I learned today:

What did I read, watch, or listen to?

Daily Summary Cues

  Where did I go?

  Who did I interact with?

  How did people, my location, or the weather impact me?

  Something that made me happy:

  Any changes brewing?

Daily Summary: (free write)

Health Notes:
Physical Symptoms: Breakfast:

                                   Lunch:

                                   Dinner:

Exercise: Snacks:

Water:
Weight:

Daily Start

Date: Current time:

How did I sleep?

What did I think or feel when I woke up?

Energy Level: 1 - 2 - 3 - 4 - 5 - 6 - 7 - 8 - 9 - 10

What am I interested in or excited about?

What did I get stuck on yesterday?

What progress am I proud of right now?

Is anything blocking my progress? What is it?

Things to do brain dump:

What is one thing I will definitely achieve today?

What is one thing I would love to do today?

Gratitude:
1.
2.
3.

Notes and Plans:

Daily End

Date: Current time:

What went well today?

What needs improvement?

Something I learned today:

What did I read, watch, or listen to?

Daily Summary Cues

Where did I go?

Who did I interact with?

How did people, my location, or the weather impact me?

Something that made me happy:

Any changes brewing?

Daily Summary: (free write)

Health Notes:
Physical Symptoms: Breakfast:

                                    Lunch:

                                    Dinner:
Exercise:
                                    Snacks:

Water:
Weight:

Daily Start

Date: Current time:

How did I sleep?

What did I think or feel when I woke up?

Energy Level: 1 - 2 - 3 - 4 - 5 - 6 - 7 - 8 - 9 - 10

What am I interested in or excited about?

What did I get stuck on yesterday?

What progress am I proud of right now?

Is anything blocking my progress? What is it?

Things to do brain dump:

What is one thing I will definitely achieve today?

What is one thing I would love to do today?

Gratitude:
1.
2.
3.

Notes and Plans:

Daily End

Date: Current time:

What went well today?

What needs improvement?

Something I learned today:

What did I read, watch, or listen to?

Daily Summary Cues

Where did I go?

Who did I interact with?

How did people, my location, or the weather impact me?

Something that made me happy:

Any changes brewing?

Daily Summary: (free write)

Health Notes:
Physical Symptoms:

Breakfast:

Lunch:

Dinner:

Exercise:

Snacks:

Water:
Weight:

Daily Start

Date: Current time:

How did I sleep?

What did I think or feel when I woke up?

Energy Level: 1 - 2 - 3 - 4 - 5 - 6 - 7 - 8 - 9 - 10

What am I interested in or excited about?

What did I get stuck on yesterday?

What progress am I proud of right now?

Is anything blocking my progress? What is it?

Things to do brain dump:

What is one thing I will definitely achieve today?

What is one thing I would love to do today?

Gratitude:
1.
2.
3.

Notes and Plans:

Daily End

Date: Current time:

What went well today?

What needs improvement?

Something I learned today:

What did I read, watch, or listen to?

Daily Summary Cues

Where did I go?

Who did I interact with?

How did people, my location, or the weather impact me?

Something that made me happy:

Any changes brewing?

Daily Summary: (free write)

Health Notes:
Physical Symptoms: Breakfast:

                                         Lunch:

                                         Dinner:

Exercise:
                                         Snacks:

Water:
Weight:

Daily Start

Date: Current time:

How did I sleep?

What did I think or feel when I woke up?

Energy Level: 1 - 2 - 3 - 4 - 5 - 6 - 7 - 8 - 9 - 10

What am I interested in or excited about?

What did I get stuck on yesterday?

What progress am I proud of right now?

Is anything blocking my progress? What is it?

Things to do brain dump:

What is one thing I will definitely achieve today?

What is one thing I would love to do today?

Gratitude:
1.
2.
3.

Notes and Plans:

Daily End

Date: Current time:

What went well today?

What needs improvement?

Something I learned today:

What did I read, watch, or listen to?

Daily Summary Cues

Where did I go?

Who did I interact with?

How did people, my location, or the weather impact me?

Something that made me happy:

Any changes brewing?

Daily Summary: (free write)

Health Notes:
Physical Symptoms: Breakfast:

                                    Lunch:

                                    Dinner:

Exercise:
                                    Snacks:

Water:
Weight:

Daily Start

Date: Current time:

How did I sleep?

What did I think or feel when I woke up?

Energy Level: 1 - 2 - 3 - 4 - 5 - 6 - 7 - 8 - 9 - 10

What am I interested in or excited about?

What did I get stuck on yesterday?

What progress am I proud of right now?

Is anything blocking my progress? What is it?

Things to do brain dump:

What is one thing I will definitely achieve today?

What is one thing I would love to do today?

Gratitude:
1.
2.
3.

Notes and Plans:

Daily End

Date: Current time:

What went well today?

What needs improvement?

Something I learned today:

What did I read, watch, or listen to?

Daily Summary Cues

Where did I go?

Who did I interact with?

How did people, my location, or the weather impact me?

Something that made me happy:

Any changes brewing?

Daily Summary: (free write)

Health Notes:
Physical Symptoms:

Breakfast:

Lunch:

Dinner:

Exercise:

Snacks:

Water:
Weight:

Daily Start

Date: Current time:

How did I sleep?

What did I think or feel when I woke up?

Energy Level: 1 - 2 - 3 - 4 - 5 - 6 - 7 - 8 - 9 - 10

What am I interested in or excited about?

What did I get stuck on yesterday?

What progress am I proud of right now?

Is anything blocking my progress? What is it?

Things to do brain dump:

What is one thing I will definitely achieve today?

What is one thing I would love to do today?

Gratitude:
1.
2.
3.

Notes and Plans:

Daily End

Date: Current time:

What went well today?

What needs improvement?

Something I learned today:

What did I read, watch, or listen to?

Daily Summary Cues

- Where did I go?
- Who did I interact with?
- How did people, my location, or the weather impact me?
- Something that made me happy:
- Any changes brewing?

Daily Summary: (free write)

Health Notes:
Physical Symptoms: Breakfast:

                                   Lunch:

                                   Dinner:
Exercise:
                                   Snacks:

Water:
Weight:

Daily Start

Date: Current time:

How did I sleep?

What did I think or feel when I woke up?

Energy Level: 1 - 2 - 3 - 4 - 5 - 6 - 7 - 8 - 9 - 10

What am I interested in or excited about?

What did I get stuck on yesterday?

What progress am I proud of right now?

Is anything blocking my progress? What is it?

Things to do brain dump:

What is one thing I will definitely achieve today?

What is one thing I would love to do today?

Gratitude:
1.
2.
3.

Notes and Plans:

Daily End

Date: Current time:

What went well today?

What needs improvement?

Something I learned today:

What did I read, watch, or listen to?

Daily Summary Cues

Where did I go?

Who did I interact with?

How did people, my location, or the weather impact me?

Something that made me happy:

Any changes brewing?

Daily Summary: (free write)

Health Notes:
Physical Symptoms:

Breakfast:

Lunch:

Dinner:

Exercise:

Snacks:

Water:
Weight:

Daily Start

Date: Current time:

How did I sleep?

What did I think or feel when I woke up?

Energy Level: 1 - 2 - 3 - 4 - 5 - 6 - 7 - 8 - 9 - 10

What am I interested in or excited about?

What did I get stuck on yesterday?

What progress am I proud of right now?

Is anything blocking my progress? What is it?

Things to do brain dump:

What is one thing I will definitely achieve today?

What is one thing I would love to do today?

Gratitude:
1.
2.
3.

Notes and Plans:

Daily End

Date: Current time:

What went well today?

What needs improvement?

Something I learned today:

What did I read, watch, or listen to?

Daily Summary Cues
- Where did I go?
- Who did I interact with?
- How did people, my location, or the weather impact me?
- Something that made me happy:
- Any changes brewing?

Daily Summary: (free write)

Health Notes:
Physical Symptoms: Breakfast:

                                         Lunch:

                                         Dinner:
Exercise:
                                         Snacks:

Water:
Weight:

Daily Start

Date: Current time:

How did I sleep?

What did I think or feel when I woke up?

Energy Level: 1 - 2 - 3 - 4 - 5 - 6 - 7 - 8 - 9 - 10

What am I interested in or excited about?

What did I get stuck on yesterday?

What progress am I proud of right now?

Is anything blocking my progress? What is it?

Things to do brain dump:

What is one thing I will definitely achieve today?

What is one thing I would love to do today?

Gratitude:
1.
2.
3.

Notes and Plans:

Daily End

Date: Current time:

What went well today?

What needs improvement?

Something I learned today:

What did I read, watch, or listen to?

Daily Summary Cues

Where did I go?

Who did I interact with?

How did people, my location, or the weather impact me?

Something that made me happy:

Any changes brewing?

Daily Summary: (free write)

Health Notes:
Physical Symptoms: Breakfast:

Lunch:

Dinner:

Exercise: Snacks:

Water:
Weight:

Daily Start

Date: Current time:

How did I sleep?

What did I think or feel when I woke up?

Energy Level: 1 - 2 - 3 - 4 - 5 - 6 - 7 - 8 - 9 - 10

What am I interested in or excited about?

What did I get stuck on yesterday?

What progress am I proud of right now?

Is anything blocking my progress? What is it?

Things to do brain dump:

What is one thing I will definitely achieve today?

What is one thing I would love to do today?

Gratitude:
1.
2.
3.

Notes and Plans:

Daily End

Date: Current time:

What went well today?

What needs improvement?

Something I learned today:

What did I read, watch, or listen to?

Daily Summary Cues

Where did I go?

Who did I interact with?

How did people, my location, or the weather impact me?

Something that made me happy:

Any changes brewing?

Daily Summary: (free write)

Health Notes:
Physical Symptoms:

Exercise:

Water:
Weight:

Breakfast:

Lunch:

Dinner:

Snacks:

Daily Start

Date: Current time:

How did I sleep?

What did I think or feel when I woke up?

Energy Level: 1 - 2 - 3 - 4 - 5 - 6 - 7 - 8 - 9 - 10

What am I interested in, or excited about?

What did I get stuck on yesterday?

What progress am I proud of right now?

Is anything blocking my progress? What is it?

Things to do brain dump:

What is one thing I will definitely achieve today?

What is one thing I would love to do today?

Gratitude:
1.
2.
3.

Notes and Plans:

Daily End

Date: Current time:

What went well today?

What needs improvement?

Something I learned today:

What did I read, watch, or listen to?

Daily Summary Cues

Where did I go?

Who did I interact with?

How did people, my location, or the weather impact me?

Something that made me happy:

Any changes brewing?

Daily Summary: (free write)

Health Notes:
Physical Symptoms: Breakfast:

                                     Lunch:

                                     Dinner:

Exercise:
                                     Snacks:

Water:
Weight:

Daily Start

Date: Current time:

How did I sleep?

What did I think or feel when I woke up?

Energy Level: 1 - 2 - 3 - 4 - 5 - 6 - 7 - 8 - 9 - 10

What am I interested in, or excited about?

What did I get stuck on yesterday?

What progress am I proud of right now?

Is anything blocking my progress? What is it?

Things to do brain dump:

What is one thing I will definitely achieve today?

What is one thing I would love to do today?

Gratitude:
1.
2.
3.

Notes and Plans:

Daily End

Date: Current time:

What went well today?

What needs improvement?

Something I learned today:

What did I read, watch, or listen to?

Daily Summary Cues

Where did I go?

Who did I interact with?

How did people, my location, or the weather impact me?

Something that made me happy:

Any changes brewing?

Daily Summary: (free write)

Health Notes:
Physical Symptoms:

Breakfast:

Lunch:

Dinner:

Exercise:

Snacks:

Water:
Weight:

Daily Start

Date: Current time:

How did I sleep?

What did I think or feel when I woke up?

Energy Level: 1 - 2 - 3 - 4 - 5 - 6 - 7 - 8 - 9 - 10

What am I interested in or excited about?

What did I get stuck on yesterday?

What progress am I proud of right now?

Is anything blocking my progress? What is it?

Things to do brain dump:

What is one thing I will definitely achieve today?

What is one thing I would love to do today?

Gratitude:
1.
2.
3.

Notes and Plans:

Daily End

Date: Current time:

What went well today?

What needs improvement?

Something I learned today:

What did I read, watch, or listen to?

Daily Summary Cues

Where did I go?

Who did I interact with?

How did people, my location, or the weather impact me?

Something that made me happy:

Any changes brewing?

Daily Summary: (free write)

Health Notes:
Physical Symptoms:

Breakfast:

Lunch:

Dinner:

Exercise:

Snacks:

Water:
Weight:

Daily Start

Date: Current time:

How did I sleep?

What did I think or feel when I woke up?

Energy Level: 1 - 2 - 3 - 4 - 5 - 6 - 7 - 8 - 9 - 10

What am I interested in, or excited about?

What did I get stuck on yesterday?

What progress am I proud of right now?

Is anything blocking my progress? What is it?

Things to do brain dump:

What is one thing I will definitely achieve today?

What is one thing I would love to do today?

Gratitude:
1.
2.
3.

Notes and Plans:

Daily End

Date: Current time:

What went well today?

What needs improvement?

Something I learned today:

What did I read, watch, or listen to?

Daily Summary Cues

Where did I go?

Who did I interact with?

How did people, my location, or the weather impact me?

Something that made me happy:

Any changes brewing?

Daily Summary: (free write)

Health Notes:
Physical Symptoms:

Breakfast:

Lunch:

Dinner:

Exercise:

Snacks:

Water:
Weight:

Daily Start

Date: Current time:

How did I sleep?

What did I think or feel when I woke up?

Energy Level: 1 - 2 - 3 - 4 - 5 - 6 - 7 - 8 - 9 - 10

What am I interested in or excited about?

What did I get stuck on yesterday?

What progress am I proud of right now?

Is anything blocking my progress? What is it?

Things to do brain dump:

What is one thing I will definitely achieve today?

What is one thing I would love to do today?

Gratitude:
1.
2.
3.

Notes and Plans:

Daily End

Date: Current time:

What went well today?

What needs improvement?

Something I learned today:

What did I read, watch, or listen to?

Daily Summary Cues

Where did I go?

Who did I interact with?

How did people, my location, or the weather impact me?

Something that made me happy:

Any changes brewing?

Daily Summary: (free write)

Health Notes:
Physical Symptoms:

Breakfast:

Lunch:

Dinner:

Exercise:

Snacks:

Water:
Weight:

Daily Start

Date: Current time:

How did I sleep?

What did I think or feel when I woke up?

Energy Level: 1 - 2 - 3 - 4 - 5 - 6 - 7 - 8 - 9 - 10

What am I interested in or excited about?

What did I get stuck on yesterday?

What progress am I proud of right now?

Is anything blocking my progress? What is it?

Things to do brain dump:

What is one thing I will definitely achieve today?

What is one thing I would love to do today?

Gratitude:
1.
2.
3.

Notes and Plans:

Daily End

Date: Current time:

What went well today?

What needs improvement?

Something I learned today:

What did I read, watch, or listen to?

Daily Summary Cues

Where did I go?

Who did I interact with?

How did people, my location, or the weather impact me?

Something that made me happy:

Any changes brewing?

Daily Summary: (free write)

Health Notes:
Physical Symptoms: Breakfast:

                                   Lunch:

                                   Dinner:

Exercise:
                                   Snacks:

Water:
Weight:

Daily Start

Date: Current time:

How did I sleep?

What did I think or feel when I woke up?

Energy Level: 1 - 2 - 3 - 4 - 5 - 6 - 7 - 8 - 9 - 10

What am I interested in or excited about?

What did I get stuck on yesterday?

What progress am I proud of right now?

Is anything blocking my progress? What is it?

Things to do brain dump:

What is one thing I will definitely achieve today?

What is one thing I would love to do today?

Gratitude:
1.
2.
3.

Notes and Plans:

Daily End

Date: Current time:

What went well today?

What needs improvement?

Something I learned today:

What did I read, watch, or listen to?

Daily Summary Cues

Where did I go?

Who did I interact with?

How did people, my location, or the weather impact me?

Something that made me happy:

Any changes brewing?

Daily Summary: (free write)

Health Notes:
Physical Symptoms:

Breakfast:

Lunch:

Dinner:

Exercise:

Snacks:

Water:
Weight:

Daily Start

Date: Current time:

How did I sleep?

What did I think or feel when I woke up?

Energy Level: 1 - 2 - 3 - 4 - 5 - 6 - 7 - 8 - 9 - 10

What am I interested in or excited about?

What did I get stuck on yesterday?

What progress am I proud of right now?

Is anything blocking my progress? What is it?

Things to do brain dump:

What is one thing I will definitely achieve today?

What is one thing I would love to do today?

Gratitude:
1.
2.
3.

Notes and Plans:

Daily End

Date: Current time:

What went well today?

What needs improvement?

Something I learned today:

What did I read, watch, or listen to?

Daily Summary Cues

Where did I go?

Who did I interact with?

How did people, my location, or the weather impact me?

Something that made me happy:

Any changes brewing?

Daily Summary: (free write)

Health Notes:
Physical Symptoms:

Breakfast:

Lunch:

Dinner:

Exercise:

Snacks:

Water:
Weight:

Daily Start

Date: Current time:

How did I sleep?

What did I think or feel when I woke up?

Energy Level: 1 - 2 - 3 - 4 - 5 - 6 - 7 - 8 - 9 - 10

What am I interested in or excited about?

What did I get stuck on yesterday?

What progress am I proud of right now?

Is anything blocking my progress? What is it?

Things to do brain dump:

What is one thing I will definitely achieve today?

What is one thing I would love to do today?

Gratitude:
1.
2.
3.

Notes and Plans:

Daily End

Date: Current time:

What went well today?

What needs improvement?

Something I learned today:

What did I read, watch, or listen to?

Daily Summary Cues

Where did I go?

Who did I interact with?

How did people, my location, or the weather impact me?

Something that made me happy:

Any changes brewing?

Daily Summary: (free write)

Health Notes:
Physical Symptoms: Breakfast:

                                         Lunch:

                                         Dinner:
Exercise:
                                         Snacks:

Water:
Weight:

Daily Start

Date: Current time:

How did I sleep?

What did I think or feel when I woke up?

Energy Level: 1 - 2 - 3 - 4 - 5 - 6 - 7 - 8 - 9 - 10

What am I interested in or excited about?

What did I get stuck on yesterday?

What progress am I proud of right now?

Is anything blocking my progress? What is it?

Things to do brain dump:

What is one thing I will definitely achieve today?

What is one thing I would love to do today?

Gratitude:
1.
2.
3.

Notes and Plans:

Daily End

Date: Current time:

What went well today?

What needs improvement?

Something I learned today:

What did I read, watch, or listen to?

Daily Summary Cues

Where did I go?

Who did I interact with?

How did people, my location, or the weather impact me?

Something that made me happy:

Any changes brewing?

Daily Summary: (free write)

Health Notes:
Physical Symptoms: Breakfast:

                                     Lunch:

                                     Dinner:
Exercise:
                                     Snacks:

Water:
Weight:

Daily Start

Date: Current time:

How did I sleep?

What did I think or feel when I woke up?

Energy Level: 1 - 2 - 3 - 4 - 5 - 6 - 7 - 8 - 9 - 10

What am I interested in or excited about?

What did I get stuck on yesterday?

What progress am I proud of right now?

Is anything blocking my progress? What is it?

Things to do brain dump:

What is one thing I will definitely achieve today?

What is one thing I would love to do today?

Gratitude:
1.
2.
3.

Notes and Plans:

Daily End

Date: Current time:

What went well today?

What needs improvement?

Something I learned today:

What did I read, watch, or listen to?

Daily Summary Cues

- Where did I go?
- Who did I interact with?
- How did people, my location, or the weather impact me?
- Something that made me happy:
- Any changes brewing?

Daily Summary: (free write)

Health Notes:
Physical Symptoms: Breakfast:

                                         Lunch:

                                         Dinner:

Exercise:
                                         Snacks:

Water:
Weight:

Daily Start

Date: Current time:

How did I sleep?

What did I think or feel when I woke up?

Energy Level: 1 - 2 - 3 - 4 - 5 - 6 - 7 - 8 - 9 - 10

What am I interested in or excited about?

What did I get stuck on yesterday?

What progress am I proud of right now?

Is anything blocking my progress? What is it?

Things to do brain dump:

What is one thing I will definitely achieve today?

What is one thing I would love to do today?

Gratitude:
1.
2.
3.

Notes and Plans:

Daily End

Date: Current time:

What went well today?

What needs improvement?

Something I learned today:

What did I read, watch, or listen to?

Daily Summary Cues

Where did I go?

Who did I interact with?

How did people, my location, or the weather impact me?

Something that made me happy:

Any changes brewing?

Daily Summary: (free write)

Health Notes:
Physical Symptoms: Breakfast:

                                        Lunch:

                                        Dinner:
Exercise:
                                        Snacks:

Water:
Weight:

Daily Start

Date: Current time:

How did I sleep?

What did I think or feel when I woke up?

Energy Level: 1 - 2 - 3 - 4 - 5 - 6 - 7 - 8 - 9 - 10

What am I interested in or excited about?

What did I get stuck on yesterday?

What progress am I proud of right now?

Is anything blocking my progress? What is it?

Things to do brain dump:

What is one thing I will definitely achieve today?

What is one thing I would love to do today?

Gratitude:
1.
2.
3.

Notes and Plans:

Daily End

Date: Current time:

What went well today?

What needs improvement?

Something I learned today:

What did I read, watch, or listen to?

Daily Summary Cues

Where did I go?

Who did I interact with?

How did people, my location, or the weather impact me?

Something that made me happy:

Any changes brewing?

Daily Summary: (free write)

Health Notes:
Physical Symptoms: Breakfast:

                            Lunch:

                            Dinner:

Exercise: Snacks:

Water:
Weight:

Daily Start

Date: Current time:

How did I sleep?

What did I think or feel when I woke up?

Energy Level: 1 - 2 - 3 - 4 - 5 - 6 - 7 - 8 - 9 - 10

What am I interested in or excited about?

What did I get stuck on yesterday?

What progress am I proud of right now?

Is anything blocking my progress? What is it?

Things to do brain dump:

What is one thing I will definitely achieve today?

What is one thing I would love to do today?

Gratitude:
1.
2.
3.

Notes and Plans:

Daily End

Date: Current time:

What went well today?

What needs improvement?

Something I learned today:

What did I read, watch, or listen to?

Daily Summary Cues

Where did I go?

Who did I interact with?

How did people, my location, or the weather impact me?

Something that made me happy:

Any changes brewing?

Daily Summary: (free write)

Health Notes:
Physical Symptoms:

Breakfast:

Lunch:

Dinner:

Exercise:

Snacks:

Water:
Weight:

Daily Start

Date: Current time:

How did I sleep?

What did I think or feel when I woke up?

Energy Level: 1 - 2 - 3 - 4 - 5 - 6 - 7 - 8 - 9 - 10

What am I interested in or excited about?

What did I get stuck on yesterday?

What progress am I proud of right now?

Is anything blocking my progress? What is it?

Things to do brain dump:

What is one thing I will definitely achieve today?

What is one thing I would love to do today?

Gratitude:
1.
2.
3.

Notes and Plans:

Daily End

Date: Current time:

What went well today?

What needs improvement?

Something I learned today:

What did I read, watch, or listen to?

Daily Summary Cues

Where did I go?

Who did I interact with?

How did people, my location, or the weather impact me?

Something that made me happy:

Any changes brewing?

Daily Summary: *(free write)*

Health Notes:

Physical Symptoms:

Exercise:

Water:
Weight:

Breakfast:

Lunch:

Dinner:

Snacks:

Daily Start

Date: Current time:

How did I sleep?

What did I think or feel when I woke up?

Energy Level: 1 - 2 - 3 - 4 - 5 - 6 - 7 - 8 - 9 - 10

What am I interested in, or excited about?

What did I get stuck on yesterday?

What progress am I proud of right now?

Is anything blocking my progress? What is it?

Things to do brain dump:

What is one thing I will definitely achieve today?

What is one thing I would love to do today?

Gratitude:
1.
2.
3.

Notes and Plans:

Daily End

Date: Current time:

What went well today?

What needs improvement?

Something I learned today:

What did I read, watch, or listen to?

Daily Summary Cues

Where did I go?

Who did I interact with?

How did people, my location, or the weather impact me?

Something that made me happy:

Any changes brewing?

Daily Summary: (free write)

Health Notes:
Physical Symptoms:

Breakfast:

Lunch:

Dinner:

Exercise:

Snacks:

Water:
Weight:

Daily Start

Date: Current time:

How did I sleep?

What did I think or feel when I woke up?

Energy Level: 1 - 2 - 3 - 4 - 5 - 6 - 7 - 8 - 9 - 10

What am I interested in or excited about?

What did I get stuck on yesterday?

What progress am I proud of right now?

Is anything blocking my progress? What is it?

Things to do brain dump:

What is one thing I will definitely achieve today?

What is one thing I would love to do today?

Gratitude:
1.
2.
3.

Notes and Plans:

Daily End

Date: Current time:

What went well today?

What needs improvement?

Something I learned today:

What did I read, watch, or listen to?

Daily Summary Cues

Where did I go?

Who did I interact with?

How did people, my location, or the weather impact me?

Something that made me happy:

Any changes brewing?

Daily Summary: (free write)

Health Notes:
Physical Symptoms:

Breakfast:

Lunch:

Dinner:

Exercise:

Snacks:

Water:
Weight:

Daily Start

Date: Current time:

How did I sleep?

What did I think or feel when I woke up?

Energy Level: 1 - 2 - 3 - 4 - 5 - 6 - 7 - 8 - 9 - 10

What am I interested in or excited about?

What did I get stuck on yesterday?

What progress am I proud of right now?

Is anything blocking my progress? What is it?

Things to do brain dump:

What is one thing I will definitely achieve today?

What is one thing I would love to do today?

Gratitude:
1.
2.
3.

Notes and Plans:

Daily End

Date: Current time:

What went well today?

What needs improvement?

Something I learned today:

What did I read, watch, or listen to?

Daily Summary Cues

Where did I go?

Who did I interact with?

How did people, my location, or the weather impact me?

Something that made me happy:

Any changes brewing?

Daily Summary: (free write)

Health Notes:
Physical Symptoms: Breakfast:

                                     Lunch:

                                     Dinner:
Exercise:
                                     Snacks:

Water:
Weight:

Daily Start

Date: Current time:

How did I sleep?

What did I think or feel when I woke up?

Energy Level: 1 - 2 - 3 - 4 - 5 - 6 - 7 - 8 - 9 - 10

What am I interested in, or excited about?

What did I get stuck on yesterday?

What progress am I proud of right now?

Is anything blocking my progress? What is it?

Things to do brain dump:

What is one thing I will definitely achieve today?

What is one thing I would love to do today?

Gratitude:
1.
2.
3.

Notes and Plans:

Daily End

Date: Current time:

What went well today?

What needs improvement?

Something I learned today:

What did I read, watch, or listen to?

Daily Summary Cues

Where did I go?

Who did I interact with?

How did people, my location, or the weather impact me?

Something that made me happy:

Any changes brewing?

Daily Summary: (free write)

Health Notes:
Physical Symptoms: Breakfast:

Lunch:

Dinner:

Exercise: Snacks:

Water:
Weight:

Daily Start

Date: Current time:

How did I sleep?

What did I think or feel when I woke up?

Energy Level: 1 - 2 - 3 - 4 - 5 - 6 - 7 - 8 - 9 - 10

What am I interested in or excited about?

What did I get stuck on yesterday?

What progress am I proud of right now?

Is anything blocking my progress? What is it?

Things to do brain dump:

What is one thing I will definitely achieve today?

What is one thing I would love to do today?

Gratitude:
1.
2.
3.

Notes and Plans:

Daily End

Date: Current time:

What went well today?

What needs improvement?

Something I learned today:

What did I read, watch, or listen to?

Daily Summary Cues
- Where did I go?
- Who did I interact with?
- How did people, my location, or the weather impact me?
- Something that made me happy:
- Any changes brewing?

Daily Summary: (free write)

Health Notes:
Physical Symptoms:

Exercise:

Water:
Weight:

Breakfast:

Lunch:

Dinner:

Snacks:

Daily Start

Date: Current time:

How did I sleep?

What did I think or feel when I woke up?

Energy Level: 1 - 2 - 3 - 4 - 5 - 6 - 7 - 8 - 9 - 10

What am I interested in or excited about?

What did I get stuck on yesterday?

What progress am I proud of right now?

Is anything blocking my progress? What is it?

Things to do brain dump:

What is one thing I will definitely achieve today?

What is one thing I would love to do today?

Gratitude:
1.
2.
3.

Notes and Plans:

Daily End

Date: Current time:

What went well today?

What needs improvement?

Something I learned today:

What did I read, watch, or listen to?

Daily Summary Cues

Where did I go?

Who did I interact with?

How did people, my location, or the weather impact me?

Something that made me happy:

Any changes brewing?

Daily Summary: (free write)

Health Notes:
Physical Symptoms: Breakfast:

                                     Lunch:

                                     Dinner:
Exercise:
                                     Snacks:

Water:
Weight:

Daily Start

Date: Current time:

How did I sleep?

What did I think or feel when I woke up?

Energy Level: 1 - 2 - 3 - 4 - 5 - 6 - 7 - 8 - 9 - 10

What am I interested in or excited about?

What did I get stuck on yesterday?

What progress am I proud of right now?

Is anything blocking my progress? What is it?

Things to do brain dump:

What is one thing I will definitely achieve today?

What is one thing I would love to do today?

Gratitude:
1.
2.
3.

Notes and Plans:

Daily End

Date: Current time:

What went well today?

What needs improvement?

Something I learned today:

What did I read, watch, or listen to?

Daily Summary Cues

- Where did I go?
- Who did I interact with?
- How did people, my location, or the weather impact me?
- Something that made me happy:
- Any changes brewing?

Daily Summary: (free write)

Health Notes:
Physical Symptoms: Breakfast:

                                        Lunch:

                                        Dinner:
Exercise:
                                        Snacks:

Water:
Weight:

Daily Start

Date: Current time:

How did I sleep?

What did I think or feel when I woke up?

Energy Level: 1 - 2 - 3 - 4 - 5 - 6 - 7 - 8 - 9 - 10

What am I interested in or excited about?

What did I get stuck on yesterday?

What progress am I proud of right now?

Is anything blocking my progress? What is it?

Things to do brain dump:

What is one thing I will definitely achieve today?

What is one thing I would love to do today?

Gratitude:
1.
2.
3.

Notes and Plans:

Daily End

Date: Current time:

What went well today?

What needs improvement?

Something I learned today:

What did I read, watch, or listen to?

Daily Summary Cues

Where did I go?

Who did I interact with?

How did people, my location, or the weather impact me?

Something that made me happy:

Any changes brewing?

Daily Summary: (free write)

Health Notes:
Physical Symptoms:

Breakfast:

Lunch:

Dinner:

Exercise:

Snacks:

Water:
Weight:

Daily Start

Date: Current time:

How did I sleep?

What did I think or feel when I woke up?

Energy Level: 1 - 2 - 3 - 4 - 5 - 6 - 7 - 8 - 9 - 10

What am I interested in or excited about?

What did I get stuck on yesterday?

What progress am I proud of right now?

Is anything blocking my progress? What is it?

Things to do brain dump:

What is one thing I will definitely achieve today?

What is one thing I would love to do today?

Gratitude:
1.
2.
3.

Notes and Plans:

Daily End

Date: Current time:

What went well today?

What needs improvement?

Something I learned today:

What did I read, watch, or listen to?

Daily Summary Cues

Where did I go?

Who did I interact with?

How did people, my location, or the weather impact me?

Something that made me happy:

Any changes brewing?

Daily Summary: (free write)

Health Notes:
Physical Symptoms:

Exercise:

Water:
Weight:

Breakfast:

Lunch:

Dinner:

Snacks:

Daily Start

Date: Current time:

How did I sleep?

What did I think or feel when I woke up?

Energy Level: 1 - 2 - 3 - 4 - 5 - 6 - 7 - 8 - 9 - 10

What am I interested in or excited about?

What did I get stuck on yesterday?

What progress am I proud of right now?

Is anything blocking my progress? What is it?

Things to do brain dump:

What is one thing I will definitely achieve today?

What is one thing I would love to do today?

Gratitude:
1.
2.
3.

Notes and Plans:

Daily End

Date: Current time:

What went well today?

What needs improvement?

Something I learned today:

What did I read, watch, or listen to?

Daily Summary Cues

Where did I go?

Who did I interact with?

How did people, my location, or the weather impact me?

Something that made me happy:

Any changes brewing?

Daily Summary: (free write)

Health Notes:
Physical Symptoms:

Breakfast:

Lunch:

Dinner:

Exercise:

Snacks:

Water:
Weight:

Daily Start

Date: Current time:

How did I sleep?

What did I think or feel when I woke up?

Energy Level: 1 - 2 - 3 - 4 - 5 - 6 - 7 - 8 - 9 - 10

What am I interested in or excited about?

What did I get stuck on yesterday?

What progress am I proud of right now?

Is anything blocking my progress? What is it?

Things to do brain dump:

What is one thing I will definitely achieve today?

What is one thing I would love to do today?

Gratitude:
1.
2.
3.

Notes and Plans:

Daily End

Date: Current time:

What went well today?

What needs improvement?

Something I learned today:

What did I read, watch, or listen to?

Daily Summary Cues

Where did I go?

Who did I interact with?

How did people, my location, or the weather impact me?

Something that made me happy:

Any changes brewing?

Daily Summary: (free write)

Health Notes:
Physical Symptoms: Breakfast:

                                       Lunch:

                                       Dinner:
Exercise:
                                       Snacks:

Water:
Weight:

Daily Start

Date: Current time:

How did I sleep?

What did I think or feel when I woke up?

Energy Level: 1 - 2 - 3 - 4 - 5 - 6 - 7 - 8 - 9 - 10

What am I interested in or excited about?

What did I get stuck on yesterday?

What progress am I proud of right now?

Is anything blocking my progress? What is it?

Things to do brain dump:

What is one thing I will definitely achieve today?

What is one thing I would love to do today?

Gratitude:
1.
2.
3.

Notes and Plans:

Daily End

Date: Current time:

What went well today?

What needs improvement?

Something I learned today:

What did I read, watch, or listen to?

Daily Summary Cues

Where did I go?

Who did I interact with?

How did people, my location, or the weather impact me?

Something that made me happy:

Any changes brewing?

Daily Summary: (free write)

Health Notes:
Physical Symptoms: Breakfast:

                                      Lunch:

                                      Dinner:
Exercise:
                                      Snacks:

Water:
Weight:

Daily Start

Date: Current time:

How did I sleep?

What did I think or feel when I woke up?

Energy Level: 1 - 2 - 3 - 4 - 5 - 6 - 7 - 8 - 9 - 10

What am I interested in or excited about?

What did I get stuck on yesterday?

What progress am I proud of right now?

Is anything blocking my progress? What is it?

Things to do brain dump:

What is one thing I will definitely achieve today?

What is one thing I would love to do today?

Gratitude:
1.
2.
3.

Notes and Plans:

Daily End

Date: Current time:

What went well today?

What needs improvement?

Something I learned today:

What did I read, watch, or listen to?

Daily Summary Cues

Where did I go?

Who did I interact with?

How did people, my location, or the weather impact me?

Something that made me happy:

Any changes brewing?

Daily Summary: (free write)

Health Notes:
Physical Symptoms: Breakfast:

                                             Lunch:

                                             Dinner:

Exercise: Snacks:

Water:
Weight:

Daily Start

Date: Current time:

How did I sleep?

What did I think or feel when I woke up?

Energy Level: 1 - 2 - 3 - 4 - 5 - 6 - 7 - 8 - 9 - 10

What am I interested in or excited about?

What did I get stuck on yesterday?

What progress am I proud of right now?

Is anything blocking my progress? What is it?

Things to do brain dump:

What is one thing I will definitely achieve today?

What is one thing I would love to do today?

Gratitude:
1.
2.
3.

Notes and Plans:

Daily End

Date: Current time:

What went well today?

What needs improvement?

Something I learned today:

What did I read, watch, or listen to?

Daily Summary Cues

Where did I go?

Who did I interact with?

How did people, my location, or the weather impact me?

Something that made me happy:

Any changes brewing?

Daily Summary: (free write)

Health Notes:
Physical Symptoms: Breakfast:

                                    Lunch:

                                    Dinner:

Exercise: Snacks:

Water:
Weight:

Daily Start

Date: Current time:

How did I sleep?

What did I think or feel when I woke up?

Energy Level: 1 - 2 - 3 - 4 - 5 - 6 - 7 - 8 - 9 - 10

What am I interested in or excited about?

What did I get stuck on yesterday?

What progress am I proud of right now?

Is anything blocking my progress? What is it?

Things to do brain dump:

What is one thing I will definitely achieve today?

What is one thing I would love to do today?

Gratitude:
1.
2.
3.

Notes and Plans:

Daily End

Date: Current time:

What went well today?

What needs improvement?

Something I learned today:

What did I read, watch, or listen to?

Daily Summary Cues

Where did I go?

Who did I interact with?

How did people, my location, or the weather impact me?

Something that made me happy:

Any changes brewing?

Daily Summary: (free write)

Health Notes:
Physical Symptoms: Breakfast:

                                     Lunch:

                                     Dinner:
Exercise:
                                     Snacks:

Water:
Weight:

Daily Start

Date: Current time:

How did I sleep?

What did I think or feel when I woke up?

Energy Level: 1 - 2 - 3 - 4 - 5 - 6 - 7 - 8 - 9 - 10

What am I interested in or excited about?

What did I get stuck on yesterday?

What progress am I proud of right now?

Is anything blocking my progress? What is it?

Things to do brain dump:

What is one thing I will definitely achieve today?

What is one thing I would love to do today?

Gratitude:
1.
2.
3.

Notes and Plans:

Daily End

Date: Current time:

What went well today?

What needs improvement?

Something I learned today:

What did I read, watch, or listen to?

Daily Summary Cues

Where did I go?

Who did I interact with?

How did people, my location, or the weather impact me?

Something that made me happy:

Any changes brewing?

Daily Summary: (free write)

Health Notes:
Physical Symptoms:

Breakfast:

Lunch:

Dinner:

Exercise:

Snacks:

Water:
Weight:

Daily Start

Date: Current time:

How did I sleep?

What did I think or feel when I woke up?

Energy Level: 1 - 2 - 3 - 4 - 5 - 6 - 7 - 8 - 9 - 10

What am I interested in or excited about?

What did I get stuck on yesterday?

What progress am I proud of right now?

Is anything blocking my progress? What is it?

Things to do brain dump:

What is one thing I will definitely achieve today?

What is one thing I would love to do today?

Gratitude:
1.
2.
3.

Notes and Plans:

Daily End

Date: Current time:

What went well today?

What needs improvement?

Something I learned today:

What did I read, watch, or listen to?

Daily Summary Cues

- Where did I go?
- Who did I interact with?
- How did people, my location, or the weather impact me?
- Something that made me happy:
- Any changes brewing?

Daily Summary: (free write)

Health Notes:
Physical Symptoms: Breakfast:

                                       Lunch:

                                       Dinner:
Exercise:
                                       Snacks:

Water:
Weight:

Daily Start

Date: Current time:

How did I sleep?

What did I think or feel when I woke up?

Energy Level: 1 - 2 - 3 - 4 - 5 - 6 - 7 - 8 - 9 - 10

What am I interested in or excited about?

What did I get stuck on yesterday?

What progress am I proud of right now?

Is anything blocking my progress? What is it?

Things to do brain dump:

What is one thing I will definitely achieve today?

What is one thing I would love to do today?

Gratitude:
1.
2.
3.

Notes and Plans:

Daily End

Date: Current time:

What went well today?

What needs improvement?

Something I learned today:

What did I read, watch, or listen to?

Daily Summary Cues

Where did I go?

Who did I interact with?

How did people, my location, or the weather impact me?

Something that made me happy:

Any changes brewing?

Daily Summary: (free write)

Health Notes:
Physical Symptoms:

Exercise:

Water:
Weight:

Breakfast:

Lunch:

Dinner:

Snacks:

Daily Start

Date: Current time:

How did I sleep?

What did I think or feel when I woke up?

Energy Level: 1 - 2 - 3 - 4 - 5 - 6 - 7 - 8 - 9 - 10

What am I interested in or excited about?

What did I get stuck on yesterday?

What progress am I proud of right now?

Is anything blocking my progress? What is it?

Things to do brain dump:

What is one thing I will definitely achieve today?

What is one thing I would love to do today?

Gratitude:
1.
2.
3.

Notes and Plans:

Daily End

Date: Current time:

What went well today?

What needs improvement?

Something I learned today:

What did I read, watch, or listen to?

Daily Summary Cues

Where did I go?

Who did I interact with?

How did people, my location, or the weather impact me?

Something that made me happy:

Any changes brewing?

Daily Summary: (free write)

Health Notes:
Physical Symptoms:

Breakfast:

Lunch:

Dinner:

Exercise:

Snacks:

Water:
Weight:

Daily Start

Date: Current time:

How did I sleep?

What did I think or feel when I woke up?

Energy Level: 1 - 2 - 3 - 4 - 5 - 6 - 7 - 8 - 9 - 10

What am I interested in, or excited about?

What did I get stuck on yesterday?

What progress am I proud of right now?

Is anything blocking my progress? What is it?

Things to do brain dump:

What is one thing I will definitely achieve today?

What is one thing I would love to do today?

Gratitude:
1.
2.
3.

Notes and Plans:

Daily End

Date: Current time:

What went well today?

What needs improvement?

Something I learned today:

What did I read, watch, or listen to?

Daily Summary Cues

Where did I go?

Who did I interact with?

How did people, my location, or the weather impact me?

Something that made me happy:

Any changes brewing?

Daily Summary: (free write)

Health Notes:
Physical Symptoms:

Exercise:

Water:
Weight:

Breakfast:

Lunch:

Dinner:

Snacks:

Daily Start

Date: Current time:

How did I sleep?

What did I think or feel when I woke up?

Energy Level: 1 - 2 - 3 - 4 - 5 - 6 - 7 - 8 - 9 - 10

What am I interested in or excited about?

What did I get stuck on yesterday?

What progress am I proud of right now?

Is anything blocking my progress? What is it?

Things to do brain dump:

What is one thing I will definitely achieve today?

What is one thing I would love to do today?

Gratitude:
1.
2.
3.

Notes and Plans:

Daily End

Date: Current time:

What went well today?

What needs improvement?

Something I learned today:

What did I read, watch, or listen to?

Daily Summary Cues

Where did I go?

Who did I interact with?

How did people, my location, or the weather impact me?

Something that made me happy:

Any changes brewing?

Daily Summary: (free write)

Health Notes:
Physical Symptoms: Breakfast:

Lunch:

Dinner:

Exercise:
                                       Snacks:

Water:
Weight:

Daily Start

Date: Current time:

How did I sleep?

What did I think or feel when I woke up?

Energy Level: 1 - 2 - 3 - 4 - 5 - 6 - 7 - 8 - 9 - 10

What am I interested in or excited about?

What did I get stuck on yesterday?

What progress am I proud of right now?

Is anything blocking my progress? What is it?

Things to do brain dump:

What is one thing I will definitely achieve today?

What is one thing I would love to do today?

Gratitude:
1.
2.
3.

Notes and Plans:

Daily End

Date: Current time:

What went well today?

What needs improvement?

Something I learned today:

What did I read, watch, or listen to?

Daily Summary Cues

Where did I go?

Who did I interact with?

How did people, my location, or the weather impact me?

Something that made me happy:

Any changes brewing?

Daily Summary: (free write)

Health Notes:
Physical Symptoms: Breakfast:

                                    Lunch:

                                    Dinner:

Exercise: Snacks:

Water:
Weight:

Daily Start

Date: Current time:

How did I sleep?

What did I think or feel when I woke up?

Energy Level: 1 - 2 - 3 - 4 - 5 - 6 - 7 - 8 - 9 - 10

What am I interested in or excited about?

What did I get stuck on yesterday?

What progress am I proud of right now?

Is anything blocking my progress? What is it?

Things to do brain dump:

What is one thing I will definitely achieve today?

What is one thing I would love to do today?

Gratitude:
1.
2.
3.

Notes and Plans:

Daily End

Date: Current time:

What went well today?

What needs improvement?

Something I learned today:

What did I read, watch, or listen to?

Daily Summary Cues

Where did I go?

Who did I interact with?

How did people, my location, or the weather impact me?

Something that made me happy:

Any changes brewing?

Daily Summary: (free write)

Health Notes:
Physical Symptoms:

Breakfast:

Lunch:

Dinner:

Exercise:

Snacks:

Water:
Weight:

Daily Start

Date: Current time:

How did I sleep?

What did I think or feel when I woke up?

Energy Level: 1 - 2 - 3 - 4 - 5 - 6 - 7 - 8 - 9 - 10

What am I interested in or excited about?

What did I get stuck on yesterday?

What progress am I proud of right now?

Is anything blocking my progress? What is it?

Things to do brain dump:

What is one thing I will definitely achieve today?

What is one thing I would love to do today?

Gratitude:
1.
2.
3.

Notes and Plans:

Daily End

Date: Current time:

What went well today?

What needs improvement?

Something I learned today:

What did I read, watch, or listen to?

Daily Summary Cues

Where did I go?

Who did I interact with?

How did people, my location, or the weather impact me?

Something that made me happy:

Any changes brewing?

Daily Summary: (free write)

Health Notes:
Physical Symptoms:

Breakfast:

Lunch:

Dinner:

Exercise:

Snacks:

Water:
Weight:

Daily Start

Date: Current time:

How did I sleep?

What did I think or feel when I woke up?

Energy Level: 1 - 2 - 3 - 4 - 5 - 6 - 7 - 8 - 9 - 10

What am I interested in, or excited about?

What did I get stuck on yesterday?

What progress am I proud of right now?

Is anything blocking my progress? What is it?

Things to do brain dump:

What is one thing I will definitely achieve today?

What is one thing I would love to do today?

Gratitude:
1.
2.
3.

Notes and Plans:

Daily End

Date: Current time:

What went well today?

What needs improvement?

Something I learned today:

What did I read, watch, or listen to?

Daily Summary Cues

Where did I go?

Who did I interact with?

How did people, my location, or the weather impact me?

Something that made me happy:

Any changes brewing?

Daily Summary: (free write)

Health Notes:
Physical Symptoms:

Breakfast:

Lunch:

Dinner:

Exercise:

Snacks:

Water:
Weight:

Daily Start

Date: Current time:

How did I sleep?

What did I think or feel when I woke up?

Energy Level: 1 - 2 - 3 - 4 - 5 - 6 - 7 - 8 - 9 - 10

What am I interested in or excited about?

What did I get stuck on yesterday?

What progress am I proud of right now?

Is anything blocking my progress? What is it?

Things to do brain dump:

What is one thing I will definitely achieve today?

What is one thing I would love to do today?

Gratitude:
1.
2.
3.

Notes and Plans:

Daily End

Date: Current time:

What went well today?

What needs improvement?

Something I learned today:

What did I read, watch, or listen to?

Daily Summary Cues

Where did I go?

Who did I interact with?

How did people, my location, or the weather impact me?

Something that made me happy:

Any changes brewing?

Daily Summary: (free write)

Health Notes:
Physical Symptoms: Breakfast:

                                     Lunch:

                                     Dinner:
Exercise:
                                     Snacks:

Water:
Weight:

Daily Start

Date: Current time:

How did I sleep?

What did I think or feel when I woke up?

Energy Level: 1 - 2 - 3 - 4 - 5 - 6 - 7 - 8 - 9 - 10

What am I interested in, or excited about?

What did I get stuck on yesterday?

What progress am I proud of right now?

Is anything blocking my progress? What is it?

Things to do brain dump:

What is one thing I will definitely achieve today?

What is one thing I would love to do today?

Gratitude:
1.
2.
3.

Notes and Plans:

Daily End

Date: Current time:

What went well today?

What needs improvement?

Something I learned today:

What did I read, watch, or listen to?

Daily Summary Cues

Where did I go?

Who did I interact with?

How did people, my location, or the weather impact me?

Something that made me happy:

Any changes brewing?

Daily Summary: (free write)

Health Notes:
Physical Symptoms:

Breakfast:

Lunch:

Dinner:

Exercise:

Snacks:

Water:
Weight:

Daily Start

Date: Current time:

How did I sleep?

What did I think or feel when I woke up?

Energy Level: 1 - 2 - 3 - 4 - 5 - 6 - 7 - 8 - 9 - 10

What am I interested in, or excited about?

What did I get stuck on yesterday?

What progress am I proud of right now?

Is anything blocking my progress? What is it?

Things to do brain dump:

What is one thing I will definitely achieve today?

What is one thing I would love to do today?

Gratitude:
1.
2.
3.

Notes and Plans:

Daily End

Date: Current time:

What went well today?

What needs improvement?

Something I learned today:

What did I read, watch, or listen to?

Daily Summary Cues

Where did I go?

Who did I interact with?

How did people, my location, or the weather impact me?

Something that made me happy:

Any changes brewing?

Daily Summary: (free write)

Health Notes:
Physical Symptoms: Breakfast:

                                        Lunch:

                                        Dinner:

Exercise: Snacks:

Water:
Weight:

Daily Start

Date: Current time:

How did I sleep?

What did I think or feel when I woke up?

Energy Level: 1 - 2 - 3 - 4 - 5 - 6 - 7 - 8 - 9 - 10

What am I interested in or excited about?

What did I get stuck on yesterday?

What progress am I proud of right now?

Is anything blocking my progress? What is it?

Things to do brain dump:

What is one thing I will definitely achieve today?

What is one thing I would love to do today?

Gratitude:
1.
2.
3.

Notes and Plans:

Daily End

Date: Current time:

What went well today?

What needs improvement?

Something I learned today:

What did I read, watch, or listen to?

Daily Summary Cues
- Where did I go?
- Who did I interact with?
- How did people, my location, or the weather impact me?
- Something that made me happy:
- Any changes brewing?

Daily Summary: (free write)

Health Notes:
Physical Symptoms:

Exercise:

Water:
Weight:

Breakfast:

Lunch:

Dinner:

Snacks:

Daily Start

Date: Current time:

How did I sleep?

What did I think or feel when I woke up?

Energy Level: 1 - 2 - 3 - 4 - 5 - 6 - 7 - 8 - 9 - 10

What am I interested in or excited about?

What did I get stuck on yesterday?

What progress am I proud of right now?

Is anything blocking my progress? What is it?

Things to do brain dump:

What is one thing I will definitely achieve today?

What is one thing I would love to do today?

Gratitude:
1.
2.
3.

Notes and Plans:

Daily End

Date: Current time:

What went well today?

What needs improvement?

Something I learned today:

What did I read, watch, or listen to?

Daily Summary Cues

Where did I go?

Who did I interact with?

How did people, my location, or the weather impact me?

Something that made me happy:

Any changes brewing?

Daily Summary: (free write)

Health Notes:
Physical Symptoms:

Exercise:

Water:
Weight:

Breakfast:

Lunch:

Dinner:

Snacks:

Daily Start

Date: Current time:

How did I sleep?

What did I think or feel when I woke up?

Energy Level: 1 - 2 - 3 - 4 - 5 - 6 - 7 - 8 - 9 - 10

What am I interested in, or excited about?

What did I get stuck on yesterday?

What progress am I proud of right now?

Is anything blocking my progress? What is it?

Things to do brain dump:

What is one thing I will definitely achieve today?

What is one thing I would love to do today?

Gratitude:
1.
2.
3.

Notes and Plans:

Daily End

Date: Current time:

What went well today?

What needs improvement?

Something I learned today:

What did I read, watch, or listen to?

Daily Summary Cues

Where did I go?

Who did I interact with?

How did people, my location, or the weather impact me?

Something that made me happy:

Any changes brewing?

Daily Summary: (free write)

Health Notes:
Physical Symptoms:

Exercise:

Water:
Weight:

Breakfast:

Lunch:

Dinner:

Snacks:

Daily Start

Date: Current time:

How did I sleep?

What did I think or feel when I woke up?

Energy Level: 1 - 2 - 3 - 4 - 5 - 6 - 7 - 8 - 9 - 10

What am I interested in or excited about?

What did I get stuck on yesterday?

What progress am I proud of right now?

Is anything blocking my progress? What is it?

Things to do brain dump:

What is one thing I will definitely achieve today?

What is one thing I would love to do today?

Gratitude:
1.
2.
3.

Notes and Plans:

Daily End

Date: Current time:

What went well today?

What needs improvement?

Something I learned today:

What did I read, watch, or listen to?

Daily Summary Cues

Where did I go?

Who did I interact with?

How did people, my location, or the weather impact me?

Something that made me happy:

Any changes brewing?

Daily Summary: (free write)

Health Notes:
Physical Symptoms:

Breakfast:

Lunch:

Dinner:

Exercise:

Snacks:

Water:
Weight:

Daily Start

Date: Current time:

How did I sleep?

What did I think or feel when I woke up?

Energy Level: 1 - 2 - 3 - 4 - 5 - 6 - 7 - 8 - 9 - 10

What am I interested in or excited about?

What did I get stuck on yesterday?

What progress am I proud of right now?

Is anything blocking my progress? What is it?

Things to do brain dump:

What is one thing I will definitely achieve today?

What is one thing I would love to do today?

Gratitude:
1.
2.
3.

Notes and Plans:

Daily End

Date: Current time:

What went well today?

What needs improvement?

Something I learned today:

What did I read, watch, or listen to?

Daily Summary Cues

Where did I go?

Who did I interact with?

How did people, my location, or the weather impact me?

Something that made me happy:

Any changes brewing?

Daily Summary: (free write)

Health Notes:
Physical Symptoms: Breakfast:

                                        Lunch:

                                        Dinner:
Exercise:
                                        Snacks:

Water:
Weight:

Daily Start

Date: Current time:

How did I sleep?

What did I think or feel when I woke up?

Energy Level: 1 - 2 - 3 - 4 - 5 - 6 - 7 - 8 - 9 - 10

What am I interested in or excited about?

What did I get stuck on yesterday?

What progress am I proud of right now?

Is anything blocking my progress? What is it?

Things to do brain dump:

What is one thing I will definitely achieve today?

What is one thing I would love to do today?

Gratitude:
1.
2.
3.

Notes and Plans:

Daily End

Date: Current time:

What went well today?

What needs improvement?

Something I learned today:

What did I read, watch, or listen to?

Daily Summary Cues

Where did I go?

Who did I interact with?

How did people, my location, or the weather impact me?

Something that made me happy:

Any changes brewing?

Daily Summary: (free write)

Health Notes:
Physical Symptoms: Breakfast:

                                     Lunch:

                                     Dinner:
Exercise:
                                     Snacks:

Water:
Weight:

Daily Start

Date: Current time:

How did I sleep?

What did I think or feel when I woke up?

Energy Level: 1 - 2 - 3 - 4 - 5 - 6 - 7 - 8 - 9 - 10

What am I interested in or excited about?

What did I get stuck on yesterday?

What progress am I proud of right now?

Is anything blocking my progress? What is it?

Things to do brain dump:

What is one thing I will definitely achieve today?

What is one thing I would love to do today?

Gratitude:
1.
2.
3.

Notes and Plans:

Daily End

Date: Current time:

What went well today?

What needs improvement?

Something I learned today:

What did I read, watch, or listen to?

Daily Summary Cues

Where did I go?

Who did I interact with?

How did people, my location, or the weather impact me?

Something that made me happy:

Any changes brewing?

Daily Summary: (free write)

Health Notes:
Physical Symptoms:

Breakfast:

Lunch:

Dinner:

Exercise:

Snacks:

Water:
Weight:

Daily Start

Date: Current time:

How did I sleep?

What did I think or feel when I woke up?

Energy Level: 1 - 2 - 3 - 4 - 5 - 6 - 7 - 8 - 9 - 10

What am I interested in or excited about?

What did I get stuck on yesterday?

What progress am I proud of right now?

Is anything blocking my progress? What is it?

Things to do brain dump:

What is one thing I will definitely achieve today?

What is one thing I would love to do today?

Gratitude:
1.
2.
3.

Notes and Plans:

Daily End

Date: Current time:

What went well today?

What needs improvement?

Something I learned today:

What did I read, watch, or listen to?

Daily Summary Cues

Where did I go?

Who did I interact with?

How did people, my location, or the weather impact me?

Something that made me happy:

Any changes brewing?

Daily Summary: (free write)

Health Notes:
Physical Symptoms:

Breakfast:

Lunch:

Dinner:

Exercise:

Snacks:

Water:
Weight:

Daily Start

Date: Current time:

How did I sleep?

What did I think or feel when I woke up?

Energy Level: 1 - 2 - 3 - 4 - 5 - 6 - 7 - 8 - 9 - 10

What am I interested in or excited about?

What did I get stuck on yesterday?

What progress am I proud of right now?

Is anything blocking my progress? What is it?

Things to do brain dump:

What is one thing I will definitely achieve today?

What is one thing I would love to do today?

Gratitude:
1.
2.
3.

Notes and Plans:

Daily End

Date: Current time:

What went well today?

What needs improvement?

Something I learned today:

What did I read, watch, or listen to?

Daily Summary Cues

Where did I go?

Who did I interact with?

How did people, my location, or the weather impact me?

Something that made me happy:

Any changes brewing?

Daily Summary: (free write)

Health Notes:
Physical Symptoms:

Breakfast:

Lunch:

Dinner:

Exercise:

Snacks:

Water:
Weight:

Daily Start

Date: Current time:

How did I sleep?

What did I think or feel when I woke up?

Energy Level: 1 - 2 - 3 - 4 - 5 - 6 - 7 - 8 - 9 - 10

What am I interested in, or excited about?

What did I get stuck on yesterday?

What progress am I proud of right now?

Is anything blocking my progress? What is it?

Things to do brain dump:

What is one thing I will definitely achieve today?

What is one thing I would love to do today?

Gratitude:
1.
2.
3.

Notes and Plans:

Daily End

Date: Current time:

What went well today?

What needs improvement?

Something I learned today:

What did I read, watch, or listen to?

Daily Summary Cues
- Where did I go?
- Who did I interact with?
- How did people, my location, or the weather impact me?
- Something that made me happy:
- Any changes brewing?

Daily Summary: (free write)

Health Notes:
Physical Symptoms: Breakfast:

Lunch:

Dinner:
Exercise:
Snacks:

Water:
Weight:

Daily Start

Date: Current time:

How did I sleep?

What did I think or feel when I woke up?

Energy Level: 1 - 2 - 3 - 4 - 5 - 6 - 7 - 8 - 9 - 10

What am I interested in or excited about?

What did I get stuck on yesterday?

What progress am I proud of right now?

Is anything blocking my progress? What is it?

Things to do brain dump:

What is one thing I will definitely achieve today?

What is one thing I would love to do today?

Gratitude:
1.
2.
3.

Notes and Plans:

Daily End

Date: Current time:

What went well today?

What needs improvement?

Something I learned today:

What did I read, watch, or listen to?

Daily Summary Cues

Where did I go?

Who did I interact with?

How did people, my location, or the weather impact me?

Something that made me happy:

Any changes brewing?

Daily Summary: (free write)

Health Notes:
Physical Symptoms: Breakfast:

                                       Lunch:

                                       Dinner:

Exercise:
                                       Snacks:

Water:
Weight:

Daily Start

Date: Current time:

How did I sleep?

What did I think or feel when I woke up?

Energy Level: 1 - 2 - 3 - 4 - 5 - 6 - 7 - 8 - 9 - 10

What am I interested in, or excited about?

What did I get stuck on yesterday?

What progress am I proud of right now?

Is anything blocking my progress? What is it?

Things to do brain dump:

What is one thing I will definitely achieve today?

What is one thing I would love to do today?

Gratitude:
1.
2.
3.

Notes and Plans:

Daily End

Date: Current time:

What went well today?

What needs improvement?

Something I learned today:

What did I read, watch, or listen to?

Daily Summary Cues

Where did I go?

Who did I interact with?

How did people, my location, or the weather impact me?

Something that made me happy:

Any changes brewing?

Daily Summary: (free write)

Health Notes:
Physical Symptoms:

Breakfast:

Lunch:

Dinner:

Exercise:

Snacks:

Water:
Weight:

Daily Start

Date: Current time:

How did I sleep?

What did I think or feel when I woke up?

Energy Level: 1 - 2 - 3 - 4 - 5 - 6 - 7 - 8 - 9 - 10

What am I interested in or excited about?

What did I get stuck on yesterday?

What progress am I proud of right now?

Is anything blocking my progress? What is it?

Things to do brain dump:

What is one thing I will definitely achieve today?

What is one thing I would love to do today?

Gratitude:
1.
2.
3.

Notes and Plans:

Daily End

Date: Current time:

What went well today?

What needs improvement?

Something I learned today:

What did I read, watch, or listen to?

Daily Summary Cues
- Where did I go?
- Who did I interact with?
- How did people, my location, or the weather impact me?
- Something that made me happy:
- Any changes brewing?

Daily Summary: (free write)

Health Notes:
Physical Symptoms: Breakfast:

Lunch:

Dinner:

Exercise:
Snacks:

Water:
Weight:

Daily Start

Date: Current time:

How did I sleep?

What did I think or feel when I woke up?

Energy Level: 1 - 2 - 3 - 4 - 5 - 6 - 7 - 8 - 9 - 10

What am I interested in or excited about?

What did I get stuck on yesterday?

What progress am I proud of right now?

Is anything blocking my progress? What is it?

Things to do brain dump:

What is one thing I will definitely achieve today?

What is one thing I would love to do today?

Gratitude:
1.
2.
3.

Notes and Plans:

Daily End

Date: Current time:

What went well today?

What needs improvement?

Something I learned today:

What did I read, watch, or listen to?

Daily Summary Cues

Where did I go?

Who did I interact with?

How did people, my location, or the weather impact me?

Something that made me happy:

Any changes brewing?

Daily Summary: (free write)

Health Notes:
Physical Symptoms: Breakfast:

                                      Lunch:

                                      Dinner:
Exercise:
                                      Snacks:

Water:
Weight:

Daily Start

Date: Current time:

How did I sleep?

What did I think or feel when I woke up?

Energy Level: 1 - 2 - 3 - 4 - 5 - 6 - 7 - 8 - 9 - 10

What am I interested in or excited about?

What did I get stuck on yesterday?

What progress am I proud of right now?

Is anything blocking my progress? What is it?

Things to do brain dump:

What is one thing I will definitely achieve today?

What is one thing I would love to do today?

Gratitude:
1.
2.
3.

Notes and Plans:

Daily End

Date: Current time:

What went well today?

What needs improvement?

Something I learned today:

What did I read, watch, or listen to?

Daily Summary Cues

Where did I go?

Who did I interact with?

How did people, my location, or the weather impact me?

Something that made me happy:

Any changes brewing?

Daily Summary: (free write)

Health Notes:
Physical Symptoms:

Exercise:

Water:
Weight:

Breakfast:

Lunch:

Dinner:

Snacks:

Daily Start

Date: Current time:

How did I sleep?

What did I think or feel when I woke up?

Energy Level: 1 - 2 - 3 - 4 - 5 - 6 - 7 - 8 - 9 - 10

What am I interested in or excited about?

What did I get stuck on yesterday?

What progress am I proud of right now?

Is anything blocking my progress? What is it?

Things to do brain dump:

What is one thing I will definitely achieve today?

What is one thing I would love to do today?

Gratitude:
1.
2.
3.

Notes and Plans:

Daily End

Date: Current time:

What went well today?

What needs improvement?

Something I learned today:

What did I read, watch, or listen to?

Daily Summary Cues
- Where did I go?
- Who did I interact with?
- How did people, my location, or the weather impact me?
- Something that made me happy:
- Any changes brewing?

Daily Summary: *(free write)*

Health Notes:
Physical Symptoms:

Exercise:

Water:
Weight:

Breakfast:

Lunch:

Dinner:

Snacks:

Daily Start

Date: Current time:

How did I sleep?

What did I think or feel when I woke up?

Energy Level: 1 - 2 - 3 - 4 - 5 - 6 - 7 - 8 - 9 - 10

What am I interested in, or excited about?

What did I get stuck on yesterday?

What progress am I proud of right now?

Is anything blocking my progress? What is it?

Things to do brain dump:

What is one thing I will definitely achieve today?

What is one thing I would love to do today?

Gratitude:
1.
2.
3.

Notes and Plans:

Daily End

Date: Current time:

What went well today?

What needs improvement?

Something I learned today:

What did I read, watch, or listen to?

Daily Summary Cues

Where did I go?

Who did I interact with?

How did people, my location, or the weather impact me?

Something that made me happy:

Any changes brewing?

Daily Summary: (free write)

Health Notes:
Physical Symptoms: Breakfast:

                                       Lunch:

                                       Dinner:

Exercise:
                                       Snacks:

Water:
Weight:

Daily Start

Date: Current time:

How did I sleep?

What did I think or feel when I woke up?

Energy Level: 1 - 2 - 3 - 4 - 5 - 6 - 7 - 8 - 9 - 10

What am I interested in or excited about?

What did I get stuck on yesterday?

What progress am I proud of right now?

Is anything blocking my progress? What is it?

Things to do brain dump:

What is one thing I will definitely achieve today?

What is one thing I would love to do today?

Gratitude:
1.
2.
3.

Notes and Plans:

Daily End

Date: Current time:

What went well today?

What needs improvement?

Something I learned today:

What did I read, watch, or listen to?

Daily Summary Cues

Where did I go?

Who did I interact with?

How did people, my location, or the weather impact me?

Something that made me happy:

Any changes brewing?

Daily Summary: (free write)

Health Notes:
Physical Symptoms: Breakfast:

                                        Lunch:

                                        Dinner:
Exercise:
                                        Snacks:

Water:
Weight:

Month Summaries

Month 1:
Mental:

Emotional:

Physical:

Spiritual:

Month 2:
Mental:

Emotional:

Physical:

Spiritual:

Month Summaries

Month 3:
Mental:

Emotional:

Physical:

Spiritual:

Month 4:
Mental:

Emotional:

Physical:

Spiritual:

Gratitude Prompts

It's not always easy to think of what to be grateful for, or to find that you are listing almost the same things every day. There is certainly nothing wrong with that. But here are a few ideas to help you branch out and find new things to be grateful for.

1. Things that are cold
2. Things that are warm
3. Things that are hot
4. People older than me
5. People younger than me
6. Daily conveniences
7. Things about work
8. Things about money
9. Things outside
10. Things inside
11. Things up high
12. Things down low
13. Things related to holidays
14. Things related to weekends
15. Things I saw yesterday
16. Things in my bedroom
17. Things in my kitchen
18. Special relationships
19. Things that are very small
20. Things that are very large
21. Things that I wear
22. Ways I can move my body
23. Books that have impacted me
24. Things that are sweet
25. Things that are sour
26. Things that are spicy
27. Things related to weather
28. Things hard to be thankful for
29. My gifts and talents
30. Gifts and talents of others
31. Things I can hear

1. Things in a box
2. Things in the night
3. Things related to transportation
4. Things related to my health
5. Things related to the health of others
6. Things that are red
7. Things that are orange
8. Things that are yellow
9. Things that are green
10. Things that are blue
11. Things that are purple
12. Things that are white
13. Things that are black
14. Things in shadow
15. Things in light
16. Things others might not notice
17. Traits of my favorite people
18. Things I can touch right now
19. Things I may never touch at all
20. Things that are new
21. Things that are old
22. People who are close-by
23. People who are far away
24. People I see regularly
25. People I lost contact with
26. Things on TV
27. Movies that made me think
28. Books that taught me or made me happier
29. Animals I have known
30. Things inside my home
31. Things that grow